# ANCIENT
# SECRETS OF
# SUCCESS

Evangeline has learned the greatest truth of all. Life flows in the direction of thought. If we think right, we speak right, and things turn out right. Evangeline carries a strong Holy Spirit anointing and when she steps to the microphone, you know the pastor is in the house. Her enthusiasm is contagious and it is an honor to endorse the ability of this gifted Woman of God.

BILL & DUSKA ANNIS
Author – *From Faith to Faith*
Canadian President of **Faith Christian Fellowship**


Success begins with obeying the greatest commandment, which includes loving God with our minds. So how do we love God with our mind? For the answer, I strongly recommend that you dig deeply into, *Ancient Secrets of Success*, and into your Bible, and go on a lifetime adventure of discovering and living out the *Ancient Secrets of Success* that God planned for you!

ESTHER RENNICK
Blogger - *Unashamed Woman*
**The SKY Family**


The principles of Joshua will help you find the keys to success. I highly recommend this book to bring about the needed changes in your life. God has called you to live an abundant life!

JAMES BYRD
Senior Pastor
**LifeSong** - Stockton, California

As I was reading Ancient Secrets of Success, I couldn't stop thinking of the many people who needed to hear its message. It is Ancient secrets but the approach is still fresh and new for today. This book has impacted my life and I know it will do the same for you.

PATTI ANASTASIO STEPHENSON
Singer & Songwriter
**Worship Pastor**

Evangeline Inman in her latest book, "Ancient Secrets of Success" reminds us of the intimate connection between thoughts, words and actions. She reveals how God gave these Ancient Secrets of Success to Joshua, exposes them repeatedly in the lives of other successful men and women in God's Word and encourages us to incorporate them in our daily lives.

REVEREND DARRELL A. MCLELLAN
Founding pastor of Abundant Life Christian Center
**Rivers of Restoration Ministries** - NB Canada

# ANCIENT
## SECRETS OF
# *Success*

EVANGELINE INMAN

Ancient Secrets of Success

# CONTENTS

# CHAPTER 1

## *Roots Go Deep*

JOSHUA WAS GIVEN THE SECRETS OF SUCCESS. Thousands of years ago, God spoke and guaranteed him success in every area of his life. It was conditional on his following certain guidelines. God said, "Keep this Book of the Law always on your lips; meditate on it day and night, so that you may be careful to do everything written in it. Then you will be prosperous and successful." (See Joshua 1:8 NIV.)

**GOD'S WORD**

1. Speak it (Always on your Lips)
2. Think it (Meditate day and night)
3. Do it (Careful to do everything written in it)
   = *Prosperous & Successful* (Joshua 1:8)

Joshua led God's people into their promised land. He lived life to the full. He was successful.

These secrets of success can be applied to our lives. They are as powerful and life-changing today as they were thousands of years ago.

## FREEPORT, BAHAMAS

I stepped onto the hotel balcony. The water looked like a sea of sparkling diamonds. I could feel the warmth from the sun as I reached for my sunglasses. Usually the beach relaxes me. The ocean is one of my favorite spots, but my heart ached as I watched the people walking on the white sandy beaches below me. The Grand Bahamas Island is a perfect location for relaxation, but I could feel tension crawling up my neck.

What appeared to be a door of opportunity had slammed shut in my face. I was struggling with the hurt and stinging disappointment. I felt slighted and unappreciated. Physically I was standing in a vacation dream spot, but emotionally my mind was in the dumps.

I knew these thoughts would make the hurt grow. If I continued to allow my thoughts to churn in that direction, they would destroy my joy. I made a decision to think on God's promises. I didn't want a root of bitterness planted in my heart. I began deliberately thinking on one of my favorite passages of Scripture, *"Trust in the Lord with all of your heart and don't depend on what you can see and understand, instead acknowledge God in everything you do, and He promises to direct your path."* (See Proverbs 3:5-6.)

Whenever I found myself starting to think about what had

happened, I would stop and begin repeating this Scripture. Several times during the day, my mind drifted back to the negative, but the more I persisted in aligning my thoughts with Scripture, the easier it was to stay positive.

My attitude changed, and my joy grew. I relaxed in a hammock between two palm trees and listened to the relaxing sounds of the ocean. Thankfulness welled up in my heart. Why was I discouraged when I was living in the midst of God's blessings? I determined to enjoy the good in my life.

I had to stay diligent day and night so as to not allow those hurtful thoughts to creep back into my mind. *"Why didn't they think I had the ability? It doesn't seem fair! Why did this happen to me? I would have done a great job!"* These unanswered questions filled my mind. I didn't know the answers, and it was a waste of time to focus on it. It drained my energy trying to figure it out. A depressing spirit was trying stamp out my joy.

God began to speak through the words of the Scripture I had meditated on over the last several hours. I heard Him say to my heart, *"If you really trusted me, then you would be rejoicing. You asked me to direct your steps, and I answered your prayer!"* It hit me! God was directing my steps. This closed door was an answer to my prayers. It was so simple, yet I had missed this truth.

I should be thrilled. God was leading me in the right path for my life. I should be throwing a party saying, *"Wow, I asked for direction, and God clearly gave it to me, and now I don't have to wonder what to do because it has been taken out of my hands."*

Pure joy! I didn't need to worry because God was leading my life, and He had closed the door! Man was not in control of my future. God's hand was upon my destiny and I relaxed. Because I was thinking on God's plan for my life, it was exciting! I stopped caring about man's plans. Peace filled my heart. God's Word healed my wounded feelings.

The Almighty God is leading and directing your steps. He has an incredible plan for your life and future. He will lead you in the best path for your life. Rejoice in the closed doors as much as the open doors. Don't bang down the closed doors. You can be confident God is working all things together for the good of those who love Him.

My happiness was not determined by my surroundings, but it was centered in my thoughts. I could be miserable on a dream vacation, or I could choose to be thankful and think about the blessings in my life. The secret was in my thinking.

## THOUGHT, TALK, ACTIONS

God gave Joshua three keys to success. It involved his speech, thoughts, and actions. What you think about is what you usually talk about. What you talk about you usually do. A very basic example we experience on almost a daily basis is saying, *"I'm going to the store."* You just prophesied about what you were going to do. You spoke before something happened in your future and then took action. Your words propel you toward the destination.

Joshua's thought-life was directly connected with his success in life. The same is true for each of us. Your thought-life is connected to what your future will look like, so God specifically spoke to Joshua about the importance of understanding this power. Your thinking affects your speaking, your speaking affects your actions, and your actions affect your future.

Every day we say things that become prophetic for our future, and often we don't even realize how important it is. To be successful, you will need to be diligent to take to heart these three strategies for success. Remember to put God's Word in your mouth, your mind, and your methods. This can be done through singing or speaking. Make it a habit to put God's words in your thoughts. God's instructions to Joshua were very specific, "Keep this Book of the Law always on your lips and meditate on it all day long and through the night, then you will be able to do what is right and become successful in every area of your life." (See Joshua 1:8.)

## ANCIENT SECRETS OF SUCCESS

Keep God's word in your:

1. Mouth
2. Mind
3. Methods

## NOTHING WILL OFFEND ME

Several months after I had returned from our trip to the Bahamas, I was in the middle of my personal devotions when a Scripture jumped out at me. Then Jesus said, *"Father, forgive them, for they do not know what they do"* (Luke 23:34 NKJV). Of course I had heard this Scripture many times before, but at that moment they became living words to me.

Those words began to burn in my heart. I realized that those who had hurt me didn't realize the damage they had inflicted. They didn't truly understand how their words and actions impacted my life. I thought about decisions people make who later realize the extent of the hurt they caused the people they love. If they could have grasped the full repercussions of what they were doing, they never would have done it.

In that sacred moment, I wrote a simple chorus: "Father, forgive them, for they know not what they do." It was a powerfully anointed time as I sat at my piano singing this Scripture-inspired song. I began reflecting back on every person I could think of throughout my life who had wounded me. I sang the song over them as tears flowed down my face. It was a time of cleansing and healing for me.

It was so wonderful I didn't want those moments to end. I began to sing those words over people who had barely offended me. I just wanted to stay in a place of worship a little longer.

Then I started thinking about the time I was on vacation in the Bahamas several months before. I started to sing over the people who had hurt me, but I stopped. It was apparent I didn't even have a twinge of resentment toward them any longer. I tried to mustard it up so I could continue my time of forgiveness, but I realized I didn't need to forgive them. There was nothing left to forgive.

I thought, *"Surely I need to sing this over them. What they did was much worse than what many of the people I had just sung and wept over in forgiveness had done;"* but I didn't feel an ounce of hurt over that situation.

Because I refused to think about it during that painful time, no root of bitterness had been planted in the hurt soil of my heart. I couldn't believe it. There were other people on my list who I had forgiven many times before, but because I had let my thoughts dwell on what they had done to me, a root of bitterness had sprung up strong and sturdy. It was hard to get rid of. I had to dig deeply to get the bitterness out.

It was so beautiful for me to realize that, by simply not thinking on the wrong, I was free from any bitterness and had removed the power those actions had held in my life. The Bible says, *"Great peace have they who love Your law; nothing shall offend them..."* (Psalm 119:165 AMP). The offense held no power over my emotions, because I had filled my thoughts with God's Word and purposely refused to think about how they had hurt me.

This is one of the ancient secrets of success found in God's Word. To live a life free of offense, we need to fill our thoughts with God's Word and refuse to think on the hurtful actions of others.

The truth is, we have hurt other people without realizing just how badly we have hurt them. A careless word might have pierced someone's heart, and we may not even know it. So show grace just like you would like to be shown.

Don't waste your energy or time on thinking over and over, sometimes for years on end, about hurtful words, actions, or broken promises. Think on God's Word instead, and you will be free from the bondage of bitterness and resentment.

## PEACE OF MIND

When your heart is filled with the words of Jesus, then other people's words will fade into insignificance. When you think about the beautiful words God has spoken over you, this can break the sting of hurtful words from your past. Their words stop having the power to hurt you as soon as you stop thinking about them.

God wants you to live a life filled with peace. He is the

Prince of Peace. He has designed and purposed for you to live an abundant life. He came that you might have an abundant life. He has made a way for you to live free of stress and worry, "and the peace of God, which surpasses all understanding, will guard your hearts and minds through Christ Jesus" (Philippians 4:7 NKJV).

There is something powerful about getting our minds on Jesus. His presence is always with us, but something changes within us when we recognize and honor His holy presence. God is for you and not against you! Keep looking to Jesus.

## ANCIENT SECRETS REVEALED

Joshua demonstrated a desire to stay in the presence of God. He stayed in the tent of meeting where God's presence would descend. Even after Moses finished speaking with God, Joshua stayed behind. This passion for God's presence gives us insight into his priorities.

The years pass, and Joshua is given a heavy mantle of responsibility. One of the most incredible leaders of all time is gone. Moses has passed on, and the leadership of God's people is now Joshua's. It is one thing to assume a job from someone who has done a mediocre job, but Joshua is taking over from an anointed, powerful, and influential man who saw a burning bush and heard God call him into ministry. This man had challenged Pharaoh, one of the richest and most powerful leaders of that time, and plagues came upon the land exactly as he predicted.

Moses led over a million people out of slavery, and they walked out of Egypt loaded with gold and silver. The Red Sea parted before them. He was personally given the Ten Commandments written by the finger of God, entrusted with the governance of His people, and the overseeing of the tabernacle. If that wasn't enough to convince any reader of his incredible resume, consider the fact his name is mentioned over 800 times in the Bible.

In comparing the two leaders, Joshua is mentioned three times in the New Testament, where Moses is mentioned over 100 times. During Jesus' ministry, Moses appeared, along with Elijah, on the Mount of Transfiguration and talked with Jesus. The list of how God used him is mind-boggling. It would take pages to describe the miracles that happened during Moses' ministry. It is highly probable Joshua felt at least a twinge of inadequacy when it came to taking over after Moses. It was a challenging task to fill the enormous shoes left by Moses.

## JOSHUA GIVEN KEYS TO SUCCESS

Joshua needed God to show him how to succeed. God spoke to him and gave him steps to success. Joshua was assuming a weighty responsibility as leader of the Children of Israel. Joshua needed wisdom to fulfill his new role. We now can read and follow the same concise steps that lead to his success. God was about to use Joshua to accomplish greatness. He had wonderful plans for Joshua's future, just as He has great plans for your future.

These are ancient secrets God has revealed to us in His Holy Word. How incredible that God gave steps to success. It's worth taking time to learn what the Creator of the universe has to say about being successful in life. God tells Joshua that, if he would keep the words of God in his mouth, in his mind, and in his actions, he would be successful. This is the pattern to find success.

"Keep this Book of the Law always on your lips; meditate

on it day and night, so that you may be careful to do everything written in it. Then you will be prosperous and successful" (Joshua 1:8 NIV).

## ANCIENT SECRETS OF SUCCESS

1. Speak it (Keep God's Word always on your lips.)
2. *Think on it (Meditate on God's Word day and night.)*
3. *Do it (Be careful to do everything in God's Word.)*

*– Joshua 1:8*

## BIND THEM ON OUR FOREHEADS

One way to success is to guard our thought-life. "You shall meditate on God's words day and night." (See Joshua 1:8.) The Scripture instructs us to fix God's words in our hearts and minds, and to tie them as symbols on our hands and bind them on our foreheads. (See Deuteronomy 11:18.) I will use foreheads to represent our thought-life. When we bind something, the purpose is to keep it from moving. It is wrapped tightly around the object so it will not escape. When we bind something, it restricts movement. We need to take this approach with God's Word in regard to our thoughts. Take your thought-life and bind it tightly with God's Word, so tightly it cannot escape, and do not allow negativity, pity parties, and discouraging thoughts to reign in your mind. Bind your thoughts to God's Word until there is no movement toward negative thought patterns.

I once spoke with a university student who was looking for work. When he dropped off his resume, he felt people looked at him like he was strange. I encouraged him to stop thinking those thoughts because they lead to action. They make you act with low self-confidence. That affects the way you walk and talk. I suggested that the next time he dropped off his resume to think about what a great employee he would be, to think about how it would benefit the business if they hired him. He was a hard worker, dependable, and trustworthy, and he needed to remember those facts. Thinking life-giving thoughts fill you with confidence. It allows you to walk with confidence and leave intimidation outside the door.

Guard your thoughts. Remember God is leading you in the right path for your life. Trust in the Lord and don't lean on your own understanding. In other words, don't depend on what you can see around you. Don't look at the people around you and their reactions to you. God is working and giving you favor. Remember, God has great plans for your life. Fill your mind and heart with those thoughts, and you will be lifted to new heights.

As a result of the first two steps, the next one will surely follow: "Be careful to do according to all that is written." This last part involves our actions. What we think and speak directly results in the actions we take in life. We make decisions based on our thought-life. We think it's the right course to take, and so we head down that road, and that is action.

What we think about we usually find ourselves talking about. Have you ever found yourself apologizing to someone because you keep harping on a certain subject? It's because what we think about comes out through our words. We can be talking to someone about a particular subject, yet, what we have been thinking will eventually come up. Often our words betray what is on our heart and mind.

## THINK ON GOOD THINGS

"Finally, brothers, whatever is true, whatever is noble, whatever is right, whatever is pure, whatever is lovely, whatever is admirable – if anything is excellent or praiseworthy – think about such things" (Philippians 4:8 NIV).

When you dwell on disappointments, it will make you miserable. The longer you let it simmer in your mind, the closer it comes to boiling over. You've heard the term, "It makes my blood boil." When you stew on something, it's like letting a pot of soup sit on a hot stove until it gets so hot it eventually bubbles over and make a mess. The smell of burnt food is an unpleasant odor, and negative thoughts leave the same bitter taste and the same awful smell. Stop thinking on the wrongs done to you, and, in their place, let the power of Scripture transform your life. It will bring peace and joy to your life as you engage your mind to meditate on God's words instead of the hurtful words of other people.

We should be thankful for every shut door. God is leading and guiding our lives. God has something better in store we can't always see yet. Don't concentrate on the closed door, rather, focus on how God can open the windows of Heaven and pour out a blessing beyond what you can contain! God wants us to live an abundant life, and His word is filled with divine secrets and strategies. His plans are always good. God has a great plan for your life.

## LYRICS RENEWED MY FAITH

I put my earphones on and walked out the front door of our home. I randomly grabbed a cassette tape off the bookshelf not realizing God was directing me. I walked for hours trying to sort through the overwhelming pain of a broken heart. My little boy was in Heaven, and the separation was more than I could handle. For the first time in my life, my faith was shaken to the core.

On my walk, I cried out to God for help. The pain was so intense it was hard to breathe. I could barely make it through each day. I pushed the play button and the music began. I couldn't believe what I was hearing. It was as if the entire album had been written just for me. The music and words renewed my faith.

One song talked about either way we win; whether we are healed here on Earth, or if we go to Heaven, either way we win. There is no way to lose as Christians. The words brought comfort to my heart as I walked along the side of the road in the small town where we lived.

The lyrics were powerful, and faith filled my heart as I walked with tears running down my face. Another song encouraged me to keep believing because God would see me through.

The words to those songs filled my mind. I was reminded that God would walk with me through the darkest valley. The lyrics encouraged me to keep looking to Jesus, and, as I did, peace surrounded me. I was at a point of total desperation, but lyrics to a song brought hope that morning.

We can find encouragement through the books we read and the songs we listen to. We can be strengthened in our faith by inspiring sermons and heartfelt testimonies. There are many different ways and opportunities for us to fill our hearts with the truth of God's Word.

## WALKING IN THE SPIRIT

Your ability to follow God's Word is associated with what your mind is set upon. The Bible teaches that a mind set on earthly things will be hostile toward God, and that individual will be unable to submit to the Word of God. (See Romans 8:7.) Your actions line up with your thought-life. What you do is directly related to the way you think. You do it because you think it's okay, or you convince yourself it doesn't matter. However you reason it out in your mind, your actions are dictated by your thought-life.

In Romans the eighth chapter, we read that those who are controlled by the Spirit are those who think about things that please the Spirit. I have heard it said, *"All of heaven is attracted to the Jesus inside of you."* The law of attraction was explained over two thousand years ago in the writings of the Apostle Paul. Those who think on spiritual things will act in a spiritual way. Those who think about carnal things will act in a carnal way. Your thoughts are very powerful. (See Romans 8:5.)

"Therefore as you have received Christ Jesus the Lord, so walk in Him, having been firmly rooted and now being built up in Him and established in your faith, just as you were instructed, and overflowing with gratitude" (Colossians 2:6-7 NASB). Negative thoughts will wear you down, but keeping your thoughts on Jesus will build you up. Let your thoughts be rooted in the Word of God.

## BE ENCOURAGED

The Apostle Paul wrote to the church in Ephesus encouraging them to stay filled with faith even though he remained in prison. He didn't want God's holy people to allow their thoughts to be focused on the troubles he encountered but to keep their eyes on the love of God. Listen to the prayer from the heart of the Apostle for the followers of Jesus:

"When I think of all this, I fall to my knees and pray to the Father, the Creator of everything in heaven and on earth. I pray that from his glorious, unlimited resources he will empower you with inner strength through his Spirit. Then Christ will make his home in your hearts as you trust in him. Your roots will grow down into God's love and keep you strong. And may you have the power to understand, as all God's people should, how wide, how long, how high, and how deep his love is. May you experience the love of Christ, though it is too great to understand fully. Then you will be made complete with all the fullness of life and power that comes from God" (Ephesians 3:14-19 NLT).

You can live life to the full by being rooted and grounded in the love of God. Let your thoughts (your inner man) be strengthened with the power of God's Holy Spirit. Let Christ dwell in your thoughts. Your roots will be watered with the love of God that is beyond comprehension. The writer of Proverbs said it in this way, "… the godly are well rooted and bear their own fruit" (Proverbs 12:12 NLT). Your roots will go down deep and strong as you meditate on God's Holy Word. This is an ancient secret for success!

# CHAPTER 2

# Faith-Filled Thoughts

## ANCIENT SECRETS OF SUCCESS

1. Speak it (Keep God's Word always on your lips.)
2. Think it (Meditate on God's Word day and night.)
3. Do it (Be careful to do everything in God's Word.)

*– Joshua 1:8*

## MIND READERS

I am a worship leader at a 24/7 prayer and worship center. At one of our staff meeting, another worship leader told about an experience she had. As she was sitting at the piano singing, some people came in. They didn't appear to be engaged in the worship. She began thinking, *"Oh no! They hate my voice."*

After a while, they walked out. She thought, *"Oh no! They didn't like what I was singing."*

As they were leaving, they began talking to someone downstairs. They raved about their time spent in the worship center. They had a wonderful experience and especially enjoyed the music and worship.

She laughed when she heard the comments, and admitted she worried for nothing. Her imagination led her to believe a lie. Even though she is a powerful and anointed woman, it was easy to slip into the pit of negativity.

We can get into trouble when we start imaging what other people are thinking about us. It is a trap of the enemy to get us off focus on the anointing God has placed inside of us. We cannot tell what other people are thinking or feeling just by their reactions or facial expressions. We are not mind readers; only God knows a person's thoughts.

I've had the privilege of traveling across the USA and Canada for many years singing in churches. Many times after the service, the ones who sat with their arms folded were the first to say how much the service blessed them. They looked totally disengaged, and, yet, many times they expressed afterward how deeply the worship ministered to them. We can rarely tell how people feel. We do not know what other people are thinking. We need to refuse fear and, instead, think positive faith-filled thoughts.

We must all stand guard against the attacks of the enemy and keep the Helmet of Salvation firmly covering our head and the Shield of Faith covering our heart where our thoughts are produced.

The Shield of Faith is to protect us from the fiery arrows of the evil one. (See Ephesians 6:16.) The arrows the enemy throws at us are on fire, and our tongue is referred to as a fire in James

3:6. It goes on to say that the tongue is set on fire by hell. So the Shield of Faith extinguishes the fiery darts. Faith can extinguish negativity! When you talk faith, it destroys the works of the enemy.

Satan is referred to as a roaring lion in the Bible. All of these references have to do with sounds that come out of the mouth. The devil may roar and throw fiery darts at you with negative words, but God's power is greater than any force of darkness. Take up the Shield of Faith and the Sword of the Spirit, which is the Word of God. You can fight Satan's fear-filled words with faith words. You can defeat him by speaking God's Word.

We overcome with the blood of the Lamb and the word of our testimony. (See Revelation 12:11.) Words are powerful! Greater is He who is in us than he who is in the world. Regardless of what comes against you, you can overcome by the power of God's Word living inside you. You are victorious. You are a winner in Jesus Name! Keep your mind on faith-filled thoughts!

## YOUR FUTURE

What you think about and talk about will affect your future. The Children of Israel were set to possess the Promised Land. (See Numbers 13-14.) God gave them a promise of an incredible future in a land filled with abundance. After their miraculous escape from slavery in Egypt, they experienced one miracle after another. Now they stood at the entrance to their promised land. God directed Moses to send scouts out to survey the land. He sent a leader from each of the twelve tribes. They explored the land for forty days.

It was everything they had imagined and more. They brought back a single cluster of grapes so large it had to be carried on a pole between two men. They gathered samples of the pomegranates and figs. When the twelve scouts returned to camp, the people were eager to hear what they had to say. They began with the facts. There wasn't a shred of doubt this was a good land flowing with milk and honey. Everyone was amazed when they saw the bountiful fruit from the Promised Land. What a shame that their amazement turned to fear when they began talking about the negative.

Ten of the scouts began putting fear into people's imaginations. Only twelve had gone in to spy out the land; the rest of the people were relying on the report the spies brought back. If they had taken more time to talk about the good land and the blessings in the land, things would have turned out differently. If they had talked about the miracles God had performed for them in the past, then their faith would have risen, but, instead, they focused on the negative.

They began saying, "The people are powerful and huge. There are giants in the land, and the cities are thriving communities with huge fortified walls that we will never be able to take." (See Numbers 13:28.)

Caleb interrupted and started speaking faith again, "We should go up right now! We can take it!"

But ten other voices kept insisting it was impossible to conquer the territory. The people of that land were stronger, bigger, more equipped, so they spread a bad report. Instead of thinking about how big their God was, they decided to think about how big the enemy was.

## WHAT OTHERS THINK

Their imaginations got the best of them, and they said, "We feel like grasshoppers compared to them, and they feel the same way about us." (See Numbers 13:33.)

Now this is where they really headed onto a slippery slope. They had no idea what the people thought about them, but they assumed they thought they were weak as grasshoppers. Fear will take over your imagination, and you can begin to assume what other people are saying or thinking about you.

Forty years later, Rahab exposed the truth of what the people actually thought about them. She said, "We have heard how God parted the Red Sea for you and you walked on dry land. We are all afraid of you, and we are living in terror. We've heard how you destroyed the Amorite kings and their people, so it's no wonder our hearts are melted in fear, and no one has the courage to fight." (See Joshua 2:9-11.)

Notice that what the people of Jericho heard was what brought them fear. They hadn't seen the miracles, but they had heard about them. Someone had been spreading the word about the amazing things the God of Israel had done for His children. Your testimony can melt the heart of unbelievers. It was words of doubt that stopped the Israelites from taking the Promised Land forty years earlier, and it was words of miracles that terrified their enemies.

Isn't it amazing to hear what the giants on the other side of the Jordan actually thought about the Israelites? They didn't think they looked like grasshoppers. In fact, the people living in Jericho weren't even looking at them; instead, they were looking at how powerful Israel's God was who had done so many miracles for them. Don't make the mistake of sizing someone up and putting words in their mouth when you don't have a clue as to what they are actually thinking.

The first time the Children of Israel arrived at the Promised Land, they began thinking about the bad report. They ended up so scared they were weeping and crying out during the night. You need to guard your thoughts, especially at night. There is something about the dark of night that can magnify our worries and make everything seem worse. Once the sun comes out, things can seem a lot different. But the Children of Israel were beside themselves, and the bad report spread throughout the whole camp. It just went from bad to worse.

The bad report grew and multiplied. At first, the report was simply that the people were powerful and there were giants in the land. That's enough discouragement, but we know fear grows, and so does our imaginations. Ten of the spies insisted they wouldn't be able to conquer the land.

## FEAR CAN MULTIPLY

Now it's astonishing to see how fast fear and disbelief multiplied. Within just a few hours, there is a noticeable change in their speaking. It's no longer simply there are giants in the land. Listen to them now, *"I wish we would have died in Egypt, or even if we could have just died along the way in the wilderness."* (See Numbers 14:1-2.) That just doesn't make any sense. If they wanted to die, then at least take the risk and march into the Promised Land. Their thinking was so messed up they continued to exaggerate their circumstance.

Finally they blamed God saying, "God brought us to the land so we could be killed by the sword." First, they wanted to die, and then they began to blame God accusing Him of bringing them to the point of death. The reason they wouldn't go into the Promised Land is because they were afraid the giants would kill them, and, yet, death is the thing they were wishing for as they talked. The more they thought and meditated on the bad report the scouts had brought back, the more their imaginations ran away with them. It's the same way with us. When we start to worry, fear grows, and we can dream up even more things to worry about.

The Children of Israel worried about their wives and children. They feared they would be captured and marched away as plunder and slaves. Their fears kept growing the more they talked. They even wanted to get rid of Moses and pick a new leader to take them back to the place where God had miraculously delivered them. They wanted to return to the land of bondage where they had been enslaved for 400 years.

Caleb and Joshua tried to remind the people about the good and abundant land. It was a great place, and God would give it to them. They encouraged them to be confident because God was on their side. What is a land of giants compared to Pharaoh's army? What is a fortified city compared to a Red Sea rolling back so God's people could walk across? There is no comparison. If they had thought on the mighty miracles of God, they would have been bold. Instead, they concentrated on the problems facing their entrance into the Promised Land. They could have marched over rejoicing in the power of the Almighty God, but it was their thinking that got them into trouble. Their negative thinking led to words of doubt that turned to fear and ultimately rebellion against God's plan.

The fears settled into their minds and grew until their thoughts were festering with the stench of doubt. They were unwilling to enter the Promised Land because they focused on the bad report instead of God's promises. They paid more attention to the discouraging words from the spies than they did to the encouraging words of God. They focused their imagination on how strong the enemy was. Their thoughts defeated them. They lost the battle in their minds. No giant is big when compared to how big our God is.

### Faith, Not Denial

Caleb and Joshua didn't deny the people were powerful who occupied the land, but they emphasized God was on their side and anything was possible. You don't have to deny you are facing trouble. It is okay to acknowledge you have some giants in your life, but just don't focus on them; instead, meditate on the great things God has done for you.

Queen Esther didn't deny the risk to her life. She asked for prayer and fasting. Her attitude was, "... *if I perish, I perish*" (Esther 4:16 KJV). The three Hebrew children didn't deny they were facing a fiery furnace. Their response to Nebuchadnezzar was that God was able to deliver them, but, even if He didn't, they still would not bow down to his idol. (See Daniel 3.) Job didn't deny he was going through heartache and loss, but his response was, "*Though He slay me, yet will I trust and put my hope in Him.*" (See Job 13:15.) You don't have to deny you have problems to glorify God.

You can admit you are facing a giant, but keep reminding yourself that God is bigger than any problem. He is your source for healing, deliverance, protection, and provision. He is able to bring you through. God is on your side. Turn your focus on the One who loves you beyond what you can comprehend. Your Heavenly Father looks down with love and care. You are the apple of His eye. Keep realigning your heart on faith-filled thoughts!

## GOD IS PATIENT AND KIND

God keeps gently leading us along even when, like the Children of Israel, we make mistakes and hesitate at the promises of God. He keeps on guiding us along the right path for our life giving us fresh mercy designed for each new day. (See Lamentations 3:22-23.) Great is God's faithfulness to us. It goes beyond our earthly comprehension. The Scripture reminds us, "If we are faithless, He remains faithful…" (II Timothy 2:13 NKJV). When we stagger at the promises of God, still He gently leads us forward.

The children of the Israelites who left Egypt entered the Promised Land 40 years later. The mercy of God keeps on leading and guiding us towards the purpose and promises of God like a loving father with his cherished child. Don't allow wrong thinking and negative talking to delay your promises.

## CAN'T STAY QUIET

On one occasion, I was preaching about some of these same principles. I was ministering about how God had spoken to me one night while my son was at the children's hospital. I heard God saying, *"I am with you."* Over and over, I heard those words repeated, and it brought comfort. God's Word has supernatural power to heal the broken hearted.

All of a sudden, a young woman bolted up from her pew and interrupted me. I was surprised, because it was totally out of character for her. She was so excited about what God had done she couldn't contain it. She began relating how, through long months in the hospital, God had spoken to her. She had been severely ill with many complications, but the words God spoke to her became her strength. God had been with her through the dark night, and her joy was contagious. The doctors didn't give her much hope, but she was filled with faith. Now she was home and even back to work, and her heart was overflowing with gratitude.

When she began speaking, the entire congregation was moved. You could feel the shift in the atmosphere. People were encouraged by her testimony. She opened her mouth and brought faith. Her words changed the entire course of the service. One after another, people began testifying about miracles God had done in their lives. When we remember what God has done for us in the past, it will give us courage to face our future.

All over the building people stood to receive healing. Their faith was strengthened by hearing testimonies of what God had done. They were challenged to believe God. Your testimony is full of power. The enemy will try to convince you no one wants to hear your testimony. The truth is, this is how we overcome the accuser. We overcome by the blood of the Lamb and by the word of our testimony. (See Revelation 12:11.) The enemy will try to convince you to stay silent, but when you open your mouth and begin sharing what God has done for you, it will strengthen you, and strengthen those around you.

## ENCOURAGE YOURSELF

As a believer, you are an oracle of God, and you have the power and ability to decree blessings over your life and your family. Jesus said one of the keys to the kingdom was, "Whatever you bind on earth will be bound in heaven and whatever you loose on earth will be loosed in heaven." (See Matthew 16:19.) What are your words binding and loosing?

You prophesy over yourself when you speak. David set an

example when he encouraged himself in the Lord. Sometimes you have to encourage yourself and not rely on other people to bring you a good word. Go ahead and speak a good word for yourself and your family.

Think of your day and how many times you declared something before you accomplished it. Little things like, *"I am going to call my friend,"* or *"I am going to the bank."* We say and then we do. We usually speak before we act. It works the same way in your spiritual life. Start saying the things you want to see happen. Start stating your belief in the great things God has planned for your life.

## WORDS OF AGREEMENT

God has declared wonderful things over your life. As you speak words of faith, you are actually agreeing with God. Jesus came and broke the curse over your life. Jesus died on the cross, and the veil of separation was torn, so we can boldly come before the Throne. Hear the words Heaven has already spoken over you.

The question is asked in Scripture, *"Whose report will you believe?"* (See John 12:38.) We will believe the report of the Lord. Speak the report of the Lord over your life. You are more than a conqueror through Christ. You can do all things through Christ who strengthens you. If God is for you, who can stand against you? (See John 12:37-38, Romans 8:31, 37, Philippians 4:13.)

## YOUR HEART SPEAKS

"A good person produces good things from the treasury of a good heart, and an evil person produces evil things from the treasury of an evil heart. What you say flows from what is in your heart" (Luke 6:45 NLT).

What you do in life is connected to what preoccupies your mind. The decisions you make come from your thought process. The ideas you talk about are first formed by your thoughts. The Bible has specific instructions about what you think and speak and how it influences your actions. This ancient formula for success has been passed down through the Holy Scriptures for generations of believers to follow.

The state of your heart is controlled by your thoughts, and your thoughts dictate your words. It's not dependent on what is going on around you. It's what is deep on the inside; what you allow your mind to think about, and your mouth to talk about, will ultimately control your heart.

Speak praise instead of defeat. God has good plans for your life, so rejoice and trust His plan will work for good. Speak faith and fill your thoughts with faith so that you will live a life of faith. Praise God for the open doors, and praise just as loud for every closed door. If the door is closed, it is just as much God's leading as an open door. You can rejoice, because God is leading you in the right path for your life.

## WORDS OF HEALING

Sharon has been a good friend of mine for years. She is a nurse practitioner and teaches at the University of New Brunswick. She shared the following story in a book we wrote together entitled *Shine On.*

It all began with a fall, followed by an irritating pain in her back that persisted over the next several months. Shortly after, she began falling more frequently. By April of the next year, fifty-four-year-old Mamie Grant entered the hospital never to walk again. The diagnosis was A.L.S. or Amyotrophic Lateral Sclerosis. This dreadful disease is one that affects the neurons of the spinal cord, cortex, and medulla desensitizing the muscles bit by bit until the person is unable to move virtually imprisoned in their own body. Yet their mind is totally alert and intact. By the time Mamie became my patient, it had affected her diaphragm, and she had to be placed on a ventilator to maintain respirations. She had a tracheotomy and was not able to speak, but she had limited use of her hands, so writing was our primary form of communication.

It had been five months since she was diagnosed.

Mamie shed many tears. She was devastated by her illness. It had happened so quickly, and her prognosis was poor. She missed being home with her family. She felt helpless and alone.

Mamie was a Christian. Even in her sorrow and pain (and she suffered much pain) her face would beam if you spoke to her of her Lord. She found comfort in having the Scriptures read aloud or listening to her music. She gave me hope by watching her faith during this difficult time in her life.

I remember one day when Mamie was having a hard time coping. She was upset she couldn't go home with her family, and tears were falling fast down her cheeks and onto her pillow. She was shaking with anxiety, and all the medications I gave her were ineffective. She could not calm down, and her blood pressure had escalated to a dangerous level.

I was intent on stabilizing Mamie's blood pressure when an

older, black woman appeared at the door. She appeared to be at least in her seventies, and was neat and trim in her pretty, tailored suit. She paused at the doorway for a moment, and then slowly walked toward the bed singing in a barely audible voice,

*"What a friend we have in Jesus,*
*all our sins and grief to bear;*
*What a privilege to carry,*
*everything to God in prayer."*

I saw Mamie mouth the words along with her visitor, and a smile flitted across her face.

The woman stood next to the bed and, reaching out her arms, beckoned the family who were in the room to join her.

"Come pray with me," she offered.

We gathered around her bed, clasping hands, while this dear woman lifted up her heart and voice to God.

She began, "Come unto me all you who labor and are burdened, and I will give you rest." She prayed for Mamie to be blessed with strength and courage, to be filled with the beauty and presence of the Lord, and to trust him with her life. As she softly said "Amen", I opened my eyes to see Mamie's face filled with a peace and contentment that had not been there just ten minutes before.

"Mamie," I said, "Let me take your blood pressure again."

The reading came back perfectly normal.

How could this be? How could her vital signs change so drastically after a few short minutes of prayer? There is only one answer. The peace of God that passes all understanding had come to rest upon her. Paul writes, "Don't be anxious about anything, but in everything, by prayer and petitions, with thanksgiving, let your requests be made known unto God, and the peace of God, that passes all understanding shall guard your hearts and minds in Christ Jesus." He who calms the angry seas filled her troubled soul with peace, and she was able to rest quietly in His love.

I love this story because it so beautifully illustrates the promise of Isaiah 26:4. Those who keep their minds steadfast on our Heavenly Father will be kept in perfect peace. Our God is the Prince of Peace, and when we fill our minds and our mouths with His words, they can destroy stress and anxiety. He speaks peace to His people, so I will listen carefully for His words. (See Psalm 85:8.)

The words of comfort from the lips of a friend did what medical science could not accomplish. Your words can bring healing to the people around you. You have the power to lift someone up who is struggling. You have the ability to speak life to your spouse. The power in your words can inspire other people to do amazing things. This is a secret of success in living life to the full. This is the power of faith-filled thoughts!

# CHAPTER 3

## Power of Words

### ANCIENT SECRETS TO SUCCESS

1. Speak it (Keep God's Word always on your lips.)
2. Think it (Meditate on God's Word day and night.)
3. Do it (Be careful to do everything in God's Word.)

*– Joshua 1:8*

### EVEN THE LITTLE THINGS

My daughter was in grade school when she shocked me with her words. We were driving home from school when she commented about how ugly she was. I was devastated and replied, *"Don't say that! You are beautiful."*

I couldn't believe she thought of herself as ugly. She truly is beautiful inside and out. I was stunned. My heart hurt, and I tried to find words to convince her that she was absolutely beautiful. As I was grasping around trying to find just the right words to say, suddenly I heard God speak to me, *"How do you think it makes Me feel when you are always complaining about the way you look?"*

It hit me quite profoundly. I was God's daughter, and He didn't like hearing me voicing derogatory words about myself. It was an awakening realization; the horror I felt at hearing my daughter's words were just as repulsive to God when I spoke the same way about myself.

Often I spoke negative words about my own appearance complaining about being overweight. I repented and asked God to forgive me. We are children of the Most High God and should be careful what we say about ourselves. Nobody likes to hear that his child is ugly. We are made in God's image, and we belong to Him. Let our words build up and not tear down, even when we are speaking about ourselves.

It's not okay to talk down about yourself. You are not your own. You belong to God. Your body is the temple of the Holy Spirit. (See I Corinthians 6:19.)

## DON'T BE AFRAID OF THEIR WORDS

There is an interesting story found in the Old Testament about King Hezekiah. A large army was coming to destroy the Children of God. The enemy forces had conquered and plundered the countries surrounding them. They were a vast army with fearsome warriors, and King Hezekiah knew they didn't have the ability to withstand them. The enemy camped outside the walled city of Jerusalem where the Ark of the Covenant was. A delegation came to the wall to meet with some of King Hezekiah's top officials, but, instead of talking with the king's official, they began shouting insults and threats. So King Hezekiah's officials said, "*Speak to us in the Aramaic language and not in Hebrew, because we understand your language, and everyone on the wall can hear what you are saying.*" But the enemy's tactic was to fill their minds with fear. They wanted to bring doubt. Their words brought confusion. It was bad news and a bad report. (See II Kings 18:26-27.)

The enemy wanted the people of God to hear it. The enemy lifted up their voice and shouted threats so all of the people working or standing along the wall could hear these destructive words.

They brought fear and intimidation. They shouted threats about how powerful they were and how they had defeated every other nation they had invaded. They ridiculed the people's trust in God to deliver them.

King Hezekiah was frightened. He tore his clothes and covered himself in sackcloth before going to the house of the Lord. He sought God's guidance. He sent men over to Isaiah the Prophet to get a word from God.

Isaiah's response startles me when I think about the terrifying situation they were facing. One of the most powerful armies has surrounded their city. They were ruthless and equipped with the finest of war weaponry. The Prophet Isaiah doesn't pay one ounce of attention to their skill, their equipment, or their brutality. He doesn't even mention the vast army. He focuses on the one area we all struggle with. Isaiah responds, "*This is what God says, 'Do not be afraid of the words you have heard.'*" (See II Kings 19:6.)

Think about this for a moment. Isaiah doesn't tell them not to fear the army or their weapons. He doesn't even mention the terrifying facts that an army is about to invade their land. The only thing Isaiah mentions is the words they have heard.

Apparently the words we hear can cause more fear than the actual event. Words have the power to create fear and doubt. Words are so powerful God used them to speak the world into existence. It was the words that had power to defeat them.

When we take time to think on God's Word, it has the power to raise your dreams from the dead. His words have the power to resurrect the visions and plans He has for your life.

The enemy wasn't finished yet. More intimidation came in the form of a letter from the enemy army. Now, on top of hearing their threats verbalized, Hezekiah was reading them in black and white. So, once again, he goes to the temple and lays the letter filled with threatening words on the altar of the Most High God. He took the letter and spread it before the Lord, and his prayer is recorded. He specifically prayed about 'the words' the enemy king had written him.

Then Hezekiah prayed before the Lord, and said: "O Lord God of Israel, the One who dwells between the cherubim, You are God, You alone, of all the kingdoms of the earth. You have made heaven and earth. Incline Your ear, O Lord, and hear; open Your eyes, O Lord, and see; and hear the words of Sennacherib, which he has sent to reproach the living God..." (II Kings 19:15-19 NKJV). (Emphasis added)

When Hezekiah prayed, he pointed out the words of the enemy: *"Open your eyes O, Lord, and see and hear the words."* He doesn't pray for God to look down from Heaven and see the army and their equipment with thousands of soldiers who have surrounded Jerusalem; no, he is praying about the words written and spoken.

It is important to recognize that the words of the enemy can cause defeat. Words of doubt and discouragement can send you in the wrong direction.

The words of the Holy Scriptures have the exact opposite effect. They are words of life, "… the words that I speak unto you, they are spirit, and they are life" (John 6:63 KJV). His words will refresh and strengthen your spirit. God's Holy Word will give you life, abundant life, and a life worth living. Whose words are you thinking about? Whose words will have preeminence in your life? Whose words will you give more of the real estate of your mind to? Whose words will you let build a dwelling place on the map of your heart?

King Hezekiah received deliverance for the kingdom he governed. God heard his prayer and miraculously saved them from destruction. They got up one morning to find 185,000 enemy soldiers had mysteriously died during the night. The angel of the Lord had gone through the enemy's camp and destroyed them. King Hezekiah and his army didn't have to aim one arrow. Everywhere they looked, the enemy lay dead. Victory was given to Hezekiah by the mighty hand of the Lord. God can destroy the enemies in your life. God can turn your situation around in one night. You can go to sleep at night, and the next morning the entire landscape of your life can be changed. Don't fear their words! Don't meditate or think about the negative words spoken over you.

God has spoken peace over you. Jesus said to the waves and the wind, *"Peace, be still,"* and the wind and the waves obeyed the voice of the Lord. God is still speaking peace into the storms of our lives. If you are in the midst of a turbulent time in your life, then listen for the voice of God, because He will speak peace to your heart. He is close to the broken-hearted, and He rescues those who are crushed in spirit. (See Psalm 34:18.)

The Good Shepherd will walk with you through the Valley of the Shadow of Death. He will anoint your head with oil until you are full and running over. Even in the middle of a famine, God has more than enough. In the middle of a desert He has water you can drink and never thirst again. He is the Living Water. His words will refresh you and give you hope. Listen closely to hear His voice speaking to you. God loves you and cares about what you are facing today. He will draw close to you.

## LIFE TO THE FULL

Jesus said, "The thief's purpose is to steal and kill and destroy. My purpose is to give them a rich and satisfying life" (John 10:10 NLT). One of the reasons Jesus came to Earth was to give us an abundant life. He took the curse of sin so we could live life to the full. No longer do we have to stand outside of the Holy of Holies. We are invited to come boldly before the Throne of Grace. You don't have to live a life filled with stress. Jesus is the Prince of Peace. The Psalmist wrote, "I listen carefully to what God the Lord is saying, for he speaks peace…" (Psalm 85:8 NLT).

Here is the way of peace. Think and meditate on God's promises. We can spend more time meditating on the hurtful words of other people instead of the life-giving words of Jesus. Don't waste your thought-life on negativity. We magnify God's words by thinking more about what He has spoken over us. Whenever we give more of our thought time to what others have said, then we lift their words higher than God's Word. Guard your thoughts!

It's always painful to hear when someone has spoken ill of us, but take a moment to wipe off from your feet the dust of conflict. Have you ever said anything about somebody else and later regretted it? We have all said unkind things before and later wished we could erase it. The Scripture teaches, "Do not take to heart everything people say in case you hear someone speaking bad about you. Remember the many times you have spoken bad things about other people." (See Ecclesiastes 7:21-22.) Remember, when you hear what others have said, that you, too, have said unkind remarks. Give them a little grace, the same kind of grace you would like if someone found out what you said about them.

Sometimes we aren't even offended at the moment, but, later, when we start thinking about it, then it can really irritate us. Have you ever been discussing that remark with a friend and said, *"You know, the more I think about it, the madder I get?"* Then the dissecting begins as you think of something else they might have meant. It goes from bad to worse, and the more you think about it, the bigger it all becomes. If you want peace, then refuse to think about hurtful words.

## LET IT GO OR IT WILL GROW

I was teaching on these principles at a women's Bible study group. I was speaking about how we should exalt God's Word in our life and not the words of other people. When we think over and over again about hurtful things people have said, we start placing more importance on what they said instead of what God has said. You might not even realize it, but you are exalting their words above God's Word. They may have said some negative things about you, but God has said some positive things about you in His Word. Whose word will you believe? As you meditate and think day and night on the words of God, you are placing them in their rightful place in your life.

After the class, a lady came over to thank me. She related how the teaching impacted her heart. Her mother-in-law was always saying unkind remarks that hurt her feelings. She said, *"There are some words my mother-in-law said to me 16 years ago, and when I think about it, it still makes me mad."*

She realized she was allowing her mother-in-law's words to control her happiness. God had been speaking to her on the subject before I taught on it. God was already at work in her heart, and what I said was just another confirmation.

Whatever direction we allow our thoughts to roam can develop into a habit. In other words, it forms a deep rut in our thought patterns. It becomes easier and easier for thoughts to flow in that direction because of the rut that has been created. This can be used for the positive in the same way that it can be used for the negative.

God wants to free you from the hurtful words of your past. You don't need to dwell on what someone said to you years ago. The very word 'dwell' means to make a permanent place to live. This is what happens when you continually think about their words. You make a hurtful place and build a monument, and it becomes a habitation for hurt feelings. Hurtful words can live for years. We can recite the exact phrase they used. Today is the day to let it go. You may have to let it go again tomorrow, but, at least for today, don't think about it. Those painful words only have power when you allow them to dwell in your thoughts. Think about something else. Start quoting a Scripture over and over and start thinking on that. The Scripture has power to heal you.

## TURN AWAY

"Then he turned from him toward another and said the same thing;" … (I Samuel 17:30 NKJV).

David spoke with confidence when he looked at Goliath, and it angered his oldest brother. Eliab spoke hurtful words to David and taunted him saying, *"Why did you come down here? And with whom have you left those few sheep in the wilderness? I know your pride …"* (See I Samuel 17:28.) David is speaking about God's greatness, but his brother is highlighting David's weakness.

His brother points out that David is a lowly shepherd, but he doesn't leave it there. He emphasizes David is responsible for only a few sheep. It's a blatant attempt to make David feel inferior. He implies his brothers are doing the important work on the battlefield, but David is left home with an insignificant job. And his brother just keeps on nailing him with accusations, *"I know exactly how you are. You are full of pride."* (See above reference.) He thought David had only come to see the battle.

Talk about words that wound. His brother accuses him of coming for a selfish motive. David was simply obeying his father by coming, and, even worse, was the fact David was there to deliver a gift to his brothers. What a double whammy. David is bringing fresh food from home to make his brothers more comfortable, and, instead of being thankful, his brother belittles him. David arrives carrying approximately 30-40 pounds of roasted grain and 10 loaves of bread. He is also loaded down with 10 wedges of cheese for the captain of their division. His whole visit was planned with the intent to benefit his brothers, and to even give them favor with the captain of the army they were serving under.

The Bible says David turned away from him. Sometimes you need to turn and walk away from hurtful words. If you want to live in victory, then you will have to turn your thoughts away from what was spoken, or else those harmful words will destroy your hopes and dreams. Change your posture and turn in the opposite direction of those damaging thoughts that can ruin your life.

## ON THE BRINK OF VICTORY

David is on the brink of a victory that will forever change his life. He will move from obscurity to being celebrated everywhere he goes. If he had stayed there defending himself, he might have missed killing the giant. He could have felt sorry for himself and sulked off into a corner, but then he might possibly have missed a life-changing opportunity. What if those insulting words had distracted him? Be careful not to get trapped into arguments.

King Saul heard about David's bold statements of fighting Goliath and sent for him. David stood before the king because he kept his thoughts on the greatness of God. His words reveal his thoughts. His attitude was, *"How dare this giant defy the armies of the living God?"*

Goliath was the one who should have been terrified. David didn't meditate on what the enemy could do, instead he thought about what God could do. Compared to how big his God was, the giant was small.

King Saul gave David a bronze helmet for his head, a sword, and a warrior's outfit, but David declined the offer. The helmet would have covered his head. He didn't need to put on the negative thoughts of Saul's army. People may want to give you a piece of their mind, but refuse to put on other people's negative thoughts.

King Saul and his army had been paralyzed with fear for 40 days. They went out each day and listened to the taunts of Goliath. The more they listened to him, the more their terror increased. David had been alone tending sheep and listening to God speaking to his heart. Who you are listening to will affect your attitude. Faith comes by hearing the Word of God. Fear comes from listening to the enemy.

The garment King Saul wanted to give him didn't fit well. It felt uncomfortable. And sometimes when we get around people who are filled with negativity, it can feel uncomfortable. Refuse to dress yourself in other people's garments of intimidation, fear, and negative thoughts. Focus on God's words, and shut out the threats of the enemy.

God wants to use you to accomplish great things. You can kill giants in your life through the power of Jesus. You can turn away from the negative comments of other people. You can turn your thoughts away and refuse to wear their garments of intimidation. You can rise above it and walk away. You are called to greater things than wasting your time trying to defend yourself from every negative thing someone says.

## DON'T WASTE YOUR TIME

I listened to a cook show celebrity being interviewed on national television. The host was asking how she defended herself from the people who were saying she wasn't a good cook. I loved her attitude. She didn't have time to respond or read what her critics were saying. She was too busy shooting television shows, producing lines of cookware, and publishing cookbooks. She didn't have the time to stop and try to defend herself. They wasted their time attacking her, while she was using her time to produce all kinds of products that were enriching her life as well as that of the consumers who loved her shows. She had the same kind of attitude David did. Don't pay attention to hurtful accusations. Turn away from Eliab like David did.

God wants to speak revelation and inspiration and patterns and plans of how to accomplish the goals you have in your life. You have more important things to do than to get into arguments with other people trying to defend yourself. People's opinions change as quickly as the weather. Don't base your life on what other people are thinking about you. Base your decision on what God is thinking about you. They may make a few hurtful comments, but just ignore it, and let it pass off of you like water off a duck's back.

Get on with the important thing God has designed for your life. You have a calling to fulfill. You have a great destiny, and you don't want to get trapped trying to convince Eliab of your abilities or your right motives. If you get into a debate with him, then you might miss your moment with Goliath.

Let Eliab say whatever he wants to say, and don't waste your time trying to convince him otherwise. When the giant is lying on the ground, then you won't have to convince Eliab. Everyone, including Eliab, will see God's hand upon you. Do what God has called you to do, and the results will speak for themselves. Run like David toward the giant. He didn't walk, instead, he ran toward Goliath. When God begins to move through you, then others will notice. They will have to stop talking about your inabilities when everyone else is talking about the miracle of the slain giant.

Jesus is the answer for everything. If we meditate on God's words, they will change our ordinary life into a life of abundance and successful living according to God's plan. God has destined you for greatness. Run toward your calling. Paul the Apostle wrote, "...but one thing I do, forgetting those things which are behind and reaching forward to those things which are ahead, I press toward the goal for the prize of the upward call of God in Christ Jesus" (Philippians 3:13-14 NKJV). Press forward. Run ahead! You have important things to accomplish. Don't get sidetracked by Eliab.

# CHAPTER 4

## Treasured Thoughts

THE SHEPHERDS HEADED QUICKLY TOWARD Bethlehem and found Mary, Joseph, and baby Jesus. They bowed in awe before the manger sharing their experience with an angelic host. The entire sky was filled with angels telling of the birth of the Savior of the World. Many people heard about the shepherds' experience. Some wondered and others were astonished, but Mary had a completely different attitude. Mary treasured in her heart what the shepherds said. She pondered on the words the angels had told the shepherds. (See Luke 2:16-19.) She used the secret of meditating on the promises of the Lord.

The same occurrence happened in the second chapter of Acts when the Holy Spirit was poured out. The reaction was similar. Some wondered, some mocked, but many accepted and received the gift that came down from heaven. The same is true for all of us today. The gifts God has poured into our lives can be treasured or scorned. His words can take root in our hearts, or the enemy can come in and steal away the dreams God has given.

Mary is an example to us all. We can hear amazing stories of what God has done, and it can astound us, but we need to go from being entertained to pondering, meditating, and treasuring it in our hearts. When we hear God speaking and directing us, we need to take the time to let His promises soak into our hearts. What are you treasuring in your heart? What are you holding dear?

Mary pondered these miracles in her heart, and she was able to experience a life of great victories and be sustained through hardships. The treasure in her heart propelled her through the exciting days of watching Jesus perform miracles. What she pondered in her heart saw her through the dark days of the crucifixion and the pain of watching her son being crucified. It was with her during the celebration of His resurrection, and, once again, at the pain of separation when He ascended up to Heaven. If you will treasure God's Word in your heart, it will see you through triumph, and it will comfort you through tragedies. It's like building your house on a rock that endures the storms of life.

## THOUGHTS OF HEALING

The woman with the issue of blood pushed through the crowd. She had been sick for twelve years and had spent all her money on doctors. She could have been discouraged, but, instead, she had heard about Jesus, and she was filled with hope. The reason she had the boldness to interrupt Jesus was because of her thought process. She thought, *"If I can just touch the hem of His garment, then I know I will be healed."* (See Mark 5:21-

34.) If she would have thought about the crowd of people and their reactions, she might have hesitated and missed her miracle opportunity, but her thoughts were on the power of Jesus, and it propelled her into action.

It wasn't even her turn. Jesus was in the middle of going to pray for a child whose father was an official of the synagogue. The important people who surrounded Jesus didn't intimidate her. Her thoughts and her eyes were on the power of Jesus. She pushed in and took hold of a miracle. She talked herself into taking actions of faith. She didn't think about the crowds. She didn't think about the disciples and their opinions. She just thought about what would happen if she could touch the fringe of His garment.

What she thought about changed her life forever. She was made whole, and Jesus sought her out. She was brought to the front again, this time to stand whole and complete and hear Jesus say, *"Daughter, your faith has made you whole. Go in peace because your suffering has ended."(See above reference.)* She, who had been scorned because of her sickness, heard Jesus call her "daughter." The little girl who was dying was important because of whose daughter she was, but now Jesus leveled the playing field because this woman, who had been an outcast, was the daughter of the most important man who ever walked on Earth. She was the daughter of the King of Kings and Lord of Lords! She had a right to interrupt because of who she was. She was a child of God!

Know your rights. Remember who you are and think about the benefits of being a child of God. The Psalmist wrote, "Don't forget the benefits of the Lord." (See Psalm 103:2.) What we think about will result in what actions we take in life. We are the only ones who can choose to treasure in our hearts the promises God has given us.

## WHO ARE YOU LISTENING TO?

The lies of the enemy are subtle. It started in the Garden of Eden, and he has continued whispering accusations and questioning God's Word. Whenever we go through a hardship, the devil steps right up and starts a campaign of spreading doubt.

Sometimes he will say, *"Why did this happen to you? God must not love you anymore."*

"If you were really a Christian, this wouldn't have happened to you."

The liar questions God's love for us, then he starts to question God's sovereignty. *"If God was really in control, He would never let this happen to you. How could a loving father allow this?"*

The devil comes immediately and starts planting seeds of fear and doubt into our hearts. What we believe about why something happened to us can become more painful than what actually happened. This is a tactic of the enemy.

If you will turn your ears to Heaven, then you will hear God's truth about the event. The lies of the enemy bring torment, but the truth of God will give you joy in the midst of sorrow. God's voice will draw you to Him. You are His beloved child, and He will speak peace and comfort to your soul. Discern between the voices and choose to only listen to what God is saying. Rebuke the other voices and turn your ear to listen closely to what God is saying to you.

The enemy whispers, *"God is not reliable, and you have to*

*protect yourself.*" The lies are vicious because they go against the words of God. The cycle begins of our relying on our own strength instead of God's power. This is a horrible trap. The walls we build to try and defend ourselves end up as our own prison bars. Without realizing it, we try to do what only God can do. He alone sits on the throne of supreme sovereignty. You are not your own source. God is your source. He is your comfort, provider, protector, deliverer, strong tower, counselor, healer, and everything you need. Align your life to what God says.

Ask God to reveal anything that is a lie. What wrong assumptions do you have regarding your past? God's Word holds the answers to all of these questions. Ask God to speak truth into your heart. Replace the lies with God's truth.

We can demolish strongholds through the divine power God gives. We have supernatural power available to us. The war of the mind is not fought with human wisdom but through the mighty power of God. Through Christ we are able to bring down the stronghold of wrong thinking that has exalted itself above the knowledge of God. We are able through the power of God to bring every thought into captivity. (See II Corinthians 10:3-5.) Don't repeat the lies of the enemy. Your circumstances might truly be what the enemy has reminded you of, but start proclaiming change in Jesus Name. Open your mouth and speak words of faith!

## TEMPTATION OF JESUS

It was a marvelous occasion. John baptized Jesus in the Jordan River, then the heavens opened and a voice said, "This is my beloved Son in whom I am well pleased." (See Matthew 3:13-17.) It was the voice of the Father speaking over His child. This is what

God's voice sounds like. He rejoices over His children. This is how it sounds when God speaks. You are His beloved child, and in you He is well pleased. He rejoices over you.

Within just a few verses, another voice is heard. It is the voice of the devil, and he said, "If you are God's son, then turn these stones to bread. If you are God's son, then throw yourself down and the angels will protect you." (See Matthew 4:1-6.)

The accuser questioned Jesus about what God had spoken over His life. Heaven said, *"This is my beloved son,"* but the devil started with, *"If you really are the Son of God ..."*

We experience this same turmoil. We hear God's voice, and then we hear the enemy's voice. Whenever God speaks blessings and promises in our life, then very soon we will hear the voice of the deceiver. The accuser will question our rights as children of God. He will question God's promises. He will question God's provisions. He will try and make us think we can handle our problems ourselves instead of depending and trusting in the Great Provider! He is the father of all lies and will twist the truth.

We are children of the Most High God. We have rights as heirs and joint-heirs with Jesus. Step into your inheritance. Live like you know God is your Father. As a Spirit-filled believer, the Holy Spirit is leading you by His divine wisdom. The God who owns the cattle on a thousand hills is your God. He is not running out of resources. He has more than enough. He will supply your needs according to His riches in glory. (See Philippians 4:19.)

Start repeating God's Word! Proclaim the good news. "... Open wide your mouth and I (God) will fill it" (Psalms 81:10 NIV). He will fill it with power and authority to do great things.

It's always the right time to speak words filled with faith! It's always the right time to treasure God's promises deep within our hearts and thoughts.

For God so loved that He gave! You are loved! A God who knows everything about you places great value on you. We can stand with confidence with the love of our Heavenly Father wrapped around us.

## POWER THOUGHTS

The Scripture states, "For the word of God is quick, and powerful, ..." (Hebrews 4:12 KJV). It's alive and active and can easily cut through all of the hard places in our hearts. We can try to persuade someone for hours about things in their lives that need to change. Even if we convince them, it will take the power of God for them to live a holy life.

This is a spiritual battle, and we cannot rely on the "arm of the flesh." If we want to get rid of the carnal mindset, then we need to spend time listening to and digesting the words of God. Just one word from the Lord, and revelation, can break through any area of our lives.

Your thought-life is powerful. Just thinking positive thoughts will produce good results, but imagine what kind of results will happen as you meditate on the powerful Word of God. The Word of God can cut through years of resentment. The Word of God can change your life forever. God's Word is light, so it can illuminate any place in your life that is dark. It will bring clarity to every situation. As you put God's Word into your thought pattern, you will be lifted to higher heights than you can imagine.

## BIBLE BOOKSTORE SHELVES

I remember as a child standing in the living room with a toy accordion singing at the top of my lungs. I played it until the accordion ripped apart from overuse. I dreamed of traveling and singing at churches and making recordings. When I turned 16 years old, I was thrilled to be able to join a summer ministry group that toured across the United States singing. I recorded my first solo album the year I graduated from Bible college. Life began to pick up speed when I married. We had two beautiful children, and my life was full, but my desire still burned to record albums.

Life was busy, and my desire kept being shelved because of the pressures and time restraints of a young family with a seriously ill child. The desire may have lain dormant, but whenever I went into a Bible bookstore, it would rise up within me. I would look at the rows of CDs, and my heart would sink. I would think, *"All of these other people are recording; how will there be room for my songs?"*

It was depressing looking at all of the other people recording gospel music. I would think, *"There is so much worship music being written, how will anyone ever listen to the songs I am writing?"*

It wasn't just a selfish desire. I felt called of God to write and record, but it just wasn't happening. I believe the burning desire was from the Lord, so it was a double frustration.

Finally, I had a divine revelation. I was looking at it wrong. My thoughts were led by fear and not faith. I decided to change my thinking. The next time I saw rows of CDs I began going through them rejoicing. I said to myself, *"If God can do it for this person, then He can do it for me."* I began to encourage myself every time I entered a Bible bookstore. I would start praising God for using all of these people in music ministry. The bigger the store and the more row after row of CDs I saw, it would cause me to become excited. I would walk up and down the aisle saying to myself, "*Wow! Look at all these recording artists that God made a way for. God gave them the finances they needed. God gave them the right connections. God gave them the ability. God opened the doors for them, and I know He will do it for me! Hallelujah!*"

I went from discouragement to encouragement. I went from feeling sorry for myself to expecting great things in my life. My circumstances hadn't changed yet, but my attitude turned into joy. I have since recorded several albums, written over 1,000 songs, and traveled singing. What looked impossible became a reality because I started believing.

## WORRY IS WRONG MEDITATION

Worry is meditating on the negative. When someone worries, they are actually meditating on their problems. They have turned their heart and mind to their fears. Worrying is the wrong type of meditation.

All day long worriers can think about their problems. Worry can wake them up in the middle of the night. The problem goes over and over in their mind as they analyze it from every possible angle. Sometimes it even invades their dreams. It's the first thing that crosses their minds in the morning. Whatever they are worrying about is usually what they talk about. It comes up in their conversations, because it is always on their mind.

If you have ever worried, then you have already practiced meditation. If you are able to worry, then you are able to meditate. It is simply thinking and chewing something over and over in your mind. Take worry and replace it with God's powerful Word. Start thinking about miracles and testimonies, and your worry will start to diminish.

If you are a good worrier, then you have already been practicing. You have a jumpstart on meditation. Just focus your mind on God's Word instead of your problems. If you wake up in the middle of the night, begin thinking about miracles. How much more pleasant life will be when worriers become mediators of God's Holy Word. How many more favors and blessings will be recognized when people keep their minds on God's provision instead of their lack and failures.

It's easy to let our mind slip downward into the negative state of worrying, but it is an uphill victory to turn our thoughts heavenward and begin thinking on God's Word. It appears more relaxing to just stay in the worrying state, but the opposite is true. When you take control of your thoughts and turn them toward faith, then you will feel energized. Worry will drain you, but thinking on God's Word will inspire you. Worry will keep you down in the dumps, but Godly thinking will lift you to heavenly heights. It's worth the effort. Just turn your thoughts upward and don't stay down in the pit.

## HOW TO MEDITATE

Meditation is an action. I am not talking about meditation where you empty your thoughts; no, biblical meditation is just the opposite. Biblical meditation is to fill your mind with the Word of God. Biblical meditation is when you chew on God's words over and over until it completely fills your heart and your thoughts. Biblical meditation is not emptying your mind; instead, it is filling it with God's Word. It requires effort.

You can meditate by speaking or quietly declaring God's Word over your life. Singing is another great way to meditate because the melody gets rooted in your mind as the lyrics go into your thoughts; the message is deposited into your spirit. God can speak to you in a personal way as you meditate. God can reveal clear-cut plans to the very circumstances that used to worry you. He can quickly give you solutions to the problems you have been trying to work out on your own. Take your mind off your troubles and place your thoughts on the Problem Solver.

It is worth going after the riches of God. The first Psalm reminds us that those who meditate on God's Word day and night will prosper in whatever they do. There is a wealth of wisdom God wants to download to your heart. It is divine knowledge that will enable you to make profitable decisions. The goal is to listen and obey. Listen for His voice, and do exactly what He tells you to do, because then blessing will chase after you. Learning to meditate on God's Word has endless rewards.

## TRANSFORMED THINKING

You can be transformed into a new person just by changing your thoughts. The Scripture states, "Don't copy the behavior and customs of this world, but let God transform you into a new person by changing the way you think. Then you will learn to know God's will for you, which is good and pleasing and perfect" (Romans 12:2 NLT). You don't need to stay in the same ruts. You can rise above them to new heights. You can soar on wings like eagles.

When your thinking changes, then your words will change as well. Often we say, *"I spoke without thinking,"* but the truth is, we usually speak what we are thinking. What we really mean is, we spoke and revealed what we were truly thinking, and we should have considered how it might affect the person on the other end. If you will clean up your thinking through the power of the Holy Spirit, then you will automatically clean up your speaking.

## EXERCISE TO SUCCEED

A powerful exercise is to take a Scripture and think about it all week long, the same verse over and over again. Chew on those few sentences. If you catch yourself thinking about negative things, stop, and start thinking about the Scripture you have chosen for the week. If you hear yourself speaking negative words, stop, and start quoting that Scripture. If you find yourself growing anxious, stop, and start saying that Scripture out loud or even silently speaking it to yourself. It's about feeding your spirit on the Words of Life. Feast on the words of Jesus. Saturate your life with the Word of God. Determine in your heart to meditate on them day and night so you will be successful; not just in the material things of life, but until success touches every area of your life according to God's plan.

God spoke a word and the heavens and Earth were created. God's Word can create beauty out of nothing. God's Word can create amazing and beautiful things out of your life. Whose words will you listen to today? Whose words will you focus on this week? Whose words will control and direct your life?

## WHAT ARE YOU THINKING ABOUT?

What you think about you will become. The Bible says, "As a man thinks in his heart so is he." (See Proverbs 23:7.) What we allow to fill our minds will fill our lives. There is a saying, *"garbage in, garbage out."* If we allow garbage to fill our minds, then we can expect our lives to look like the city dump. But just imagine what a life looks like where its thoughts are filled with the Holy Word of God. You are the only one who can control what you are thinking.

Have you ever started to worry about something, and the more you thought about it, the worse it seemed? Your thinking can torment you. It can make things grow.

## YOUR MIND IS A GARDEN WHERE THINGS GROW

Anxiety has a way of growing. Scripture states, "When my anxious thoughts multiply within me, Your consolations delight (comfort) my soul" (Psalm 94:19 NASB). What are you cultivating to grow in your life? The more we worry, the longer the list becomes of additional things to worry about.

We may start out worrying about one thing, but the more we worry, the more the problem expands until we begin to see other things to worry about that we didn't even think about in the beginning. This anonymous quote put it so perfectly, *"Your mind is a garden, and your thoughts are the seeds. You can grow flowers or you can grow weeds."*

Anxious thoughts multiply, but, the wonderful thing is, faith can multiply as well. When we turn our thoughts toward God's Word, then it is magnified in our lives. It gets bigger and our worries become smaller. Whatever you spend time thinking about will grow. This can work in our favor. The visions and dreams God has given you can grow as you take time to meditate on His Word. Your faith will grow as you spend time with God's Word.

When your faith is increased, you will be able to face 'Goliath.' David wasn't thinking about how big the giant was, instead He was thinking about how big his God was. It doesn't matter how massive your problems are, they will begin to look like specks of dust when compared to the mountain of our great God. So remember, whatever you are thinking about will grow in your life.

# CHAPTER 5
## Words of Faith

**ANCIENT SECRETS OF SUCCESS**

1. Speak it (Keep God's Word always on your lips.)
2. Think it (Meditate on God's Word day and night.)
3. Do it (Be careful to do everything in God's Word.)

*– Joshua 1:8*


**LET IT HAPPEN**

The angel told Mary the Holy Spirit would overshadow her and she would conceive. Mary's reply demonstrates how to speak in faith. Though she didn't understand how it could happen, still she said, "*… I am the handmaiden of the Lord;…*" (Luke 1:38 AMP).

She knew who she was. Her words were a prophetic utterance. Mary declared over her life that God was in control, and she would follow His plan and not her own. In those few words, she foretold that her life would be one of submission to the will of the Almighty. She aligned her words with her destiny.

Mary continues, *"Let it be according to your words."* Let it happen! Mary chose to believe God's words and place them far above what anyone else might say.

Lift up your voice as a handmaiden or a servant of the Most High God and imitate Mary's words. *"Let it happen just like Your word has said!"* Our prayer should be, *"Let it happen!"*

Mary spoke words of faith to her relative Elizabeth. *"Almighty God has done great things for me, and everyone will call me blessed."* (See Luke 1.) She began speaking words of faith before the noticeable signs of pregnancy, before the miraculous birth of Jesus, before the shepherds and wise men bowed, before she married Joseph, and before they took the trip to Bethlehem. Mary declares in faith, *"Everyone will call me blessed."* We need to pronounce blessing over ourselves so our circumstances will change.

Speak out today and agree with the Word of God that you are blessed. Live in unity with God's Word and say, *"Let it be according to your word O, God."* Open your mouth and speak words of faith!

## I AM A CHILD OF GOD

Mary's declaration of faith was powerful, *"I AM the handmaiden of the Lord."* It's important what you say after the words "I AM." This was the name of God used in the Old Testament.

*"I AM that I AM."* (See Exodus 3:12-16 KJV.) "I AM" is one of the eternal names of our God, and it is to be remembered in every generation.

When you use the words "I AM," be diligent to line it up with God's Word. Don't say, *"I am stupid,"* or *"I am an airhead."* Have reverence for God's Holy Name being cautious not to take it in vain. Follow the example of Mary and start declaring words of faith after you say the words "I AM." I AM a servant of the Most High God. I AM a child of the Most High God. I AM more than a conqueror through Christ. I AM blessed and not cursed. I AM a worshipper. I AM a follower of Jesus.

Seize the promises written for you in Scripture, and start saying, *"Let it happen according to Your word."* Make it a habit to declare God's truth over your life. *"I am chosen by God,"* or *"I am blessed through Christ's sacrifice."* Every time you start a sentence with the words I AM, check to make sure what you are speaking lines up with what God's Word says about you.

## WORDS ARE POWERFUL

Words are powerful. They have the power to change the course of your life. In the New Testament James wrote, "… if we could control our tongues, we would be perfect and could also control ourselves in every other way" (James 3:2 NLT). This is an amazing Scripture. What we allow out of our mouths will impact every aspect of our lives.

What you speak can change the course of your life. The tongue is very small, but it has a lot of power. James continues teaching and expanding on the power of the tongue and how something so small can change the entire direction of a person's life. A large horse can be turned in any direction simply by the bit in its mouth. An entire ship can change its course by a very small rudder. Our tongues may be a small part of our bodies, but it has the power and ability to turn our lives completely around. (See James 3:2-10.) Faith can move mountains of fear, defeat, failure, and doubt. Open up your mouth and keep speaking words of faith to any problem in your path.

## KEYBOARDS AND FEARS

I was a teenager when I started playing keyboards in the band at our church. One of the first times I was scheduled to play for the Bible college choir, the church was packed. The sanctuary main floor and balcony were filled. My family, friends, and classmates were all there. I was scared I would mess up the introduction or maybe forget how to play the song entirely. To make matters worse, I was on the lead instrument.

Before the service, most of the choir met in the prayer room located behind the stage area. It was still over an hour before the service began, and different friends from the choir passed by and asked if I was scared. The choir was quite large. I began admitting to several people how scared I felt. Over and over I confessed words of fear like, *"I'm scared to death!"* The more I confessed my fear, the more my fear grew until eventually my body actually began to shake. It seemed like such a big deal to me. It's hard to imagine now, but at that time in my life it was terrifying. In reality, it was just pride, and the fear of looking stupid by hitting a wrong note or messing up the song somehow.

I was raised in a Pentecostal church, and most of the time we didn't use any sheet music. The musicians played by ear, and for special choir songs the entire arrangement was memorized. I had to remember the introduction, the ending, and all the chord changes in the middle. It was a lot of pressure for someone who was a beginner. Many of the musicians at the church were very skilled, and, although they were encouraging, it was still intimidating to play in front of them. The more I confessed how scared I was, the more fear multiplied. I noticed my hands were shaking, and then my legs began to shake.

As I sat backstage, it dawned on me I needed to change my attitude. I was literally shaking with fear. I started saying to myself and to those around me that I wasn't scared in the least little bit.

One of the leaders of our church walked past. She had known me since I was a child and was a woman of great faith. When she passed by me, she asked if I was scared to play. I confidently replied, *"No, I am not scared in the least!"* She looked a little shocked.

At that moment, I was still scared, but I was speaking by faith. I began telling my friends how excited I was to play in front of everyone. It was such a great opportunity. I started thinking about how God was going to help me. I thought about the music director who chose me and trusted my musical ability.

As I kept speaking about how exciting it was to play, I actually talked myself right out of fear. During all this faith-thinking, something amazing started to happen. My legs and arms stopped shaking. By the time service started, I wasn't frightened any more. All this happened within just an hour or two. When the service began, I walked out on stage with confidence and played with boldness. It was a valuable lesson for me as a new musician to be careful what I confessed over myself.

## DECLARATIONS OF FAITH

I have been a church musician and worship leader for years. Many times before I walk out on the platform, I spend a few moments declaring some facts over myself. These are God's words, and I declare them over my ministry.

1.  When I speak or sing, it is as if God Himself is speaking through me. (I Peter 4:11)

2.  I am filled with power from heaven! (Acts 1:8)

3.  God has given me spiritual gifts. (I Peter 4:10)

4.  I am chosen, royalty, holy, and God's special possession so that I can proclaim (sing) the praises of God. (I Peter 2:9)

5.  I am crowned with loving kindness and tender mercies. (Psalm 103:4)

6.  The beauty of God and His favor is upon me. (Psalm 90:17)

7.  God's hand of blessing is upon my head. (Psalm 139:5)

I have found through the years, speaking God's Word over myself before I minister makes a world of difference. I have been able to minister with boldness as I meditate on what God's Word has spoken over me. It is so easy to fall into the trap of focusing on yourself and how you might look. Turn your focus on Jesus and walk in the authority and God-confidence that comes from spending time in His Word.

## EVERYTHING YOU NEED

God has destined you for great things. He has called you His child and brought you into His royal family. As a child of the Most High God, you have divine rights and privileges. There are some things that come just because you are part of the family. Your Heavenly Father adores you and rejoices over you with singing. Listen closely to hear God rejoicing over you.

He will be your closest friend. He will be closer than a brother. He is the lover of your soul. He is your Heavenly Father. He is the perfect fulfillment of every relationship we have in the natural. For every broken relationship, He will be the perfect completion to whatever is missing in your life. The Bible tells us that, even if your mother and father forsake you, the Lord will lift you up. He is a defender of the widow. He is a father to the fatherless. He is the defender of the orphans. He is strength for the weak. He is water to the thirsty. He is bread to the hungry. (See Psalm 27:10, Psalm 68:5, Isaiah 40:9, Isaiah 44:3, Matthew 5:6.)

To live an abundant life is to have Jesus as the center of your life. One of the keys to having a successful life is to fear God and obey His commands. The key is to make Him number one, and everything else will find its rightful place. The key is to look to Him, and you will be led in the right path. So make Him number one in your thoughts.

## GOD-GIVEN DESIRES

One of my favorite passages of Scripture always fills my heart with expectation. "For God is working in you, giving you the desire and the power to do what pleases Him" (Philippians 2:13 NLT).

Praise God! He is working in your life. He is bringing about events and situations to make us willing to do His will. Whatever you are facing today, the great Creator will design something beautiful out of it. He is filling you with the power and the ability to accomplish the ministry He has called you to complete. Regardless of what you go through, know He is equipping you for the ministry of good works. You are in training and learning from the One who holds the very source of wisdom.

Don't be distracted by the cares of this life. God is in control, and He has a great plan for your future. Don't waste precious time and energy on worry. Turn your thoughts on the One who is your help in time of trouble. He has promised to supply all your needs according to His riches in glory. Remember His promises. Talk about His provisions. Share with others the miracles God has done for you in the past, and you will be filled with courage.

The writer of Hebrews closes out his letter with a prayer for the believers, "may He equip you with all you need for doing his will. May he produce in you, through the power of Jesus Christ, every good thing that is pleasing to him..." (Hebrews 13:21 NLT). I can do everything God has called me to do because God equips me, and He is working in me to produce great things for His kingdom.

You can accomplish great things for the Kingdom because God is continuing to work in you. Your destiny is not a journey you have to travel alone. God is with you every step of the way, guiding you at every turn, and directing your path. You can do all things, not on your own strength or ability, but through Christ. (See Philippians 4:13.)

## THE FATHER'S APPROVAL

Jesus was in Jerusalem. He saw a man who had been sick for thirty-eight years. The man was lying by the pool of Bethesda where crowds of really sick people were lying beneath five covered porches. Jesus looked at the man and said, *"Stand up and take your mat and walk."* (See Mark 2:9 NIV.) The man had been paralyzed all those years, but, as soon as he heard the words of Jesus, he stood up and walked away totally healed.

The religious leaders had a problem when they saw him walking carrying his mat. Working on the Sabbath was forbidden. It is almost too ridiculous to comprehend. Those leaders totally ignored the miracle of someone walking after being bedridden for thirty-eight years. They didn't rejoice that his life had been transformed. All they concerned themselves with was punishing whoever told the man to carry his mat on the Sabbath.

Jesus didn't seem to blink an eye over their accusations. He wasn't bothered by their unkind words. He was thinking about something else entirely. He responded that His Father had already spoken over Him, and what He said was true. In other words, they could throw all kinds of insults toward him, but he wasn't going to get bent out of shape because He had the words of the Father pulsating inside. The Father had already testified about Him, and what the Father said was true.

It's the same way with you. As a child of the Most High God, He has already spoken promises and blessings over your life. You don't need to get all upset about what someone else is saying against you. The words of the Father are true, and He has spoken over you.

Don't waste your time on what other people have said. Be more concerned with what God has said about you. Don't worry about what other people think about you, instead become more concerned about what God thinks about you. In fact, Jesus pointed out to the religious leaders that they didn't care about the honor that comes from God. They were too busy trying to impress each other. Jesus said to them, *"Your approval means nothing to me,"* (John 5:41 NLT). What a great position to be in, to lose your fear of man and, instead, only have a fear of God.

The way to be happy is to constantly remind yourself what God's Word has said about you. This is a pathway to success in your emotional health and in your relationships with other people. You can reach out in love when you no longer are controlled by their opinion.

## THE CRUCIFIXION

Jesus was accused but didn't respond. Pilate was puzzled. The crowd and the Pharisees were hurling insults at Him, and, yet, Jesus didn't open His mouth to respond. He didn't defend Himself. (See Matthew 27:11-14.) He knew who He was. He was the Son of God. Pilate asked Jesus if He understood that he had power to release Him, but Jesus' response must have startled Pilate. Jesus stood before him bound and accused and answered, *"You don't have any power over me except what was given from heaven."* (See John 19:11.)

Jesus understood who held the power. The words and the insults couldn't change who He was and couldn't alter the plans of God. Jesus stood firm because He had listened to the Father's voice. Jesus didn't do anything except what He saw the Father doing. He listened to the voice and followed the Father's leading. (See John 5:19.)

When you meditate on God's Word, He will speak to your heart in a way no one else can. He will impart wisdom that goes into the deep places in your life that no one else can see. God's Word is sharp and powerful; it's like a double-edge sword that can pierce right down into the damaged areas of your heart. (See Hebrews 4:12.) It reminds me of a skilled surgeon holding a scalpel. It can delicately cut and remove the infected areas. God's Word can do laser surgery on your heart and mend places no one else would be able to touch.

God's Word is so precise it doesn't even leave a scar behind. I have met people whose lives have been changed drastically. It is absolutely amazing. When they share their testimony, it's hard to believe the gentle person speaking was once so toughened by sin. God's Word can modify your behavior until your past is unrecognizable. God can change your life so dramatically people will be astonished when they hear about your past. God's Word can renew your mind until you no longer think or speak the way you used to.

# CHAPTER 6

## *Thought Patterns*

### ANCIENT SECRETS OF SUCCESS

1.  Speak it (Keep God's Word always on your lips.)
2.  Think it (Meditate on God's Word day and night.)
3.  Do it (Be careful to do everything in God's Word.)

*– Joshua 1:8*

### HAMAN'S FOCUS DESTROYED HIM

In the book of Esther, we read about an infamous man named Haman. He was an advisor to King Xerxes, a close personal friend who was so honored that people bowed when he passed in the streets. The king promoted him above all the other princes and advanced him above all the officials in the kingdom. Life was pretty great for Haman. He was respected and admired around the palace, and his wife was by his side trying to fulfill his every wish. He was extremely wealthy with a supportive family. He was one of the most powerful officials in the empire. Life was peachy-creamy.

One day some palace officials pointed out that Mordecai didn't bow when he passed by. Haman hadn't even noticed before, but now it irritated him. Haman made plans to annihilate the entire Jewish race because of Mordecai.

Haman made a fatal mistake. He turned his attention away from all of the good in his life and focused on something so small that he hadn't even notice until it was pointed out. Now his thoughts are consumed with how to get rid of Mordecai. Haman is the one eating and drinking with the king. Haman is the one with the wealth and prestige, but still he turns his focus away from the multiple blessings in his life and can only focus on this tiny irritation. I feel like screaming in the story, *"Haman, don't be an idiot. Enjoy all the blessings in your life and turn your attention away from Mordecai."* But that is not how the story ends. Haman lost everything, including his life.

He was consumed with the one thing wrong in his life, and he forgot to be thankful for all of the good. Instead of rejoicing because people bowed to him, he focused on the one who wouldn't bow. His focus made him miserable. His thought pattern destroyed him. (See Esther 3-9.)

## FOCUS ON OUR BLESSINGS

The same thing can happen in our relationships. We can have a wonderful husband or wife, but something can start to irritate us, and the more we focus on it, the unhappier we become. Soon we can't even remember all of the good things in our relationship; instead, all we can think about is what is driving us crazy. Some little problem can grow way out of proportion, and, in the end, it can destroy our relationship. Take care of what you think about. Take care of what you allow to become the focus of your thoughts. Keep a thankful heart.

One of the secrets to success is to focus on the good in your life. Be thankful for your blessings! Take time to consider all the benefits God has given to you. Don't focus on the dirty dishes; remember, God has blessed you with plenty of food to eat. Don't focus on the mountain of laundry; remember, you have a closet filled with clothes to choose from. Turn your focus on the good. God has been good to you. Let your thought pattern get in the habit of going toward thankfulness.

## BAG OF STONES

Let words of wisdom penetrate deep inside your heart, "for they bring life to those who find them, and healing to their whole body" (Proverbs 4:22 NLT). Medical science confirms that a high percentage of physical illness is related to negative emotions. Here are a few common negative emotions: anger, resentment, worry, bitterness, and, one of the biggest, unforgiveness. These emotions can make our heart beat faster and sweat start to form on our brow. Just these few physical signs show how closely related our emotional well-being is correlated to our physical health.

I've heard many different illustrations about the weight of carrying unforgiveness. One illustration is to think of carrying a large bag of marbles. Each marble represents someone who has hurt you. If you carried the bag around all day long, eventually it would get heavy. Dragging the awkward bag would hinder your progress and ability to get things done. After a long day of carrying the bag of marbles, you would be exhausted. Unfortunately, even at night you hang on to it. Imagine arranging the bag of marbles on top of your pillow and then trying to sleep. You would toss and turn trying to find a comfortable position. The unforgiveness would hinder your rest. All of this negative emotional baggage we carry makes our lives difficult. It doesn't affect the person who has hurt us.

The weight of anger, resentment, worry, and fear is too heavy for us. God's Word commands us to forgive, and it's for our own benefit, emotionally and spiritually. Resentment will slow you down from reaching your destination. Anger will hinder your progress in life. Worry will bring more stress and anxiety. Refuse to fill your mind with hurtful thoughts. It doesn't help to rehearse in your thoughts the hurtful things that have happened in your life. If you change your thought patterns, you will change your life.

Our thoughts affect our health. This truth was written thousands of years ago: "A happy heart is good medicine and a cheerful mind works healing, but a broken spirit dries up the bones" (Proverbs 17:22 AMPC). Your thoughts and your words have a direct influence on your health. We read in the Bible, "Kind words are like honey – sweet to the soul and healthy for the body" (Proverbs 16:24 NLT).

If you need a picker-upper, look for someone who has faith-filled positive words. It is hard to stay negative surrounded by faith-talking people! Stress and worry just seem to disappear when faith starts rising up. I have heard is said that fear is just negative faith. Fear is faith that something terrible is about to take place. Either way, it's the belief about an event in the future that hasn't taken place yet. Jesus said, *"Don't worry about tomorrow."*

## WHATEVER YOU DO WILL PROSPER

It will take effort to meditate on God's Word day and night. You will often have to stop and purposely change your thoughts from negativity to God's Word, but look at the promises in the first Psalm. It is worth the effort!

"Blessed [fortunate, prosperous, and favored by God] is the man who does not walk in the counsel of the wicked [following their advice and example], Nor stand in the path of sinners, Nor sit [down to rest] in the seat of scoffers (ridiculers). But his delight is in the law of the LORD, And on His law [His precepts and teachings] he [habitually] meditates day and night. And he will be like a tree firmly planted [and fed] by streams of water, Which yields its fruit in its season; Its leaf does not wither; And in whatever he does, he prospers [and comes to maturity]" (Psalm 1:1-3 AMP+).

People who make it a habit to keep their thoughts on the teachings of God all through their day and into the night will prosper in whatever they do. It's like an open-ended promise. It doesn't matter what kind of work you engage in. It sounds almost too good to be true.

Prosperity hinges on what you allow your mind to dwell on during the twenty-four hours God gives you every day. Isn't that the greatest news? It doesn't matter how much education you have. It doesn't depend on the great connections you have made through networking. It depends on what you do with your mind.

You are in control of your thoughts. No other person has the power to control what you think. You alone hold the key to your thought-life. When you give your thought-life over to the power of God's Word, then your life will blossom like never before. The Bible says you will be transformed by renewing your mind. "And be not conformed to this world: but be ye transformed by the renewing of your mind, that ye may prove what is that good, and acceptable, and perfect, will of God" (Romans 12:2 KJV). If you want to live a different life than what you are living, then begin thinking different thoughts than what you have been thinking. Start declaring God's Word to your own heart. Encourage yourself daily by thinking about God's promises to you. Just keep thinking about all the great things God has done for you in the past, and what He has promised to do in the future.

An ancient secret of success is to meditate day and night on the words of the Lord. Take your thoughts and bind them tightly to God's Word. His Word has power to change your life. Different translations of Psalm 1 use these words: blessed, happy, fortunate, prosperous, and enviable to describe the person determined to keep his mind stayed on Jesus. Positive thought patterns will lift you up.

## STAY CONNECTED

You have the power to change your life through Christ. You have the ability to transform your current circumstances. As you continually connect yourself to the Vine, you will be able to do amazing things in your life. Jesus said, *"I am the vine and you are the branches, and apart from me you can do nothing."* (See John 15:5.) But when you connect your thoughts to Jesus on a continual basis, you will soar to new heights.

You can begin this very moment. Just think on a promise from the Holy Scriptures and begin to treasure it in your heart. You can meditate on the same verse for days, and the words of God are so powerful God can reveal great new things to you. God's Word is much more powerful than we can imagine.

## YOUR CAMELS ARE COMING

Isaac was the promised son of Abraham and Sarah. A great destiny was foretold years before he was born. He was the privileged son of a wealthy father and the long awaited heir. Isaac grew into a man of faith by following the examples of his parents. He heard the stories of how his birth was a miracle. He had seen his father's devotion to Almighty God. Years pass, and it is time for Isaac to marry.

His father sends a trusted servant on a long journey to the land of Mesopotamia in search of the right spouse for his treasured son. During this time of waiting and transition in his life, Isaac goes out alone into a field. He is there to meditate. The sky unfolds in a beautiful display of the setting sun. As Isaac is meditating, he looks up and sees ten camels coming toward him. (See Genesis 24:62.)

Isaac gets away from everything distracting him. There is never an end to the list of things-to-do, and I am sure Isaac's to-do list was just as long as ours. He made a decision that meditating was important enough to go out of his way. What is riding on those camels will change his life forever. A great blessing was coming. The servant left loaded down with silver and gold jewelry. The trip was successful, and sitting on one of the ten camels is a beautiful bride handpicked for Isaac.

Rachael his wife came, and it brought him great comfort after the loss of his mother. Joy was about to return to his life. Laughter was about to enter his tent, and it came while he was meditating.

Camels represented wealth and blessings. Camels were considered the Rolls Royce of the desert. The Bible refers to camels as an indication of wealth.

While Isaac was meditating, his camels were coming toward him. He didn't have to go searching for them because they were looking for him. They were coming in his direction, down his road, and to his tent.

As you meditate on God's Word, blessings will start coming to you. You don't have to search for them, because they will be coming in your direction. Goodness and mercy will follow me all the days of my life. (See Psalm 23:6.) You don't have to look for goodness and mercy because, as a child of God, they just go wherever you go. Some blessings search you out.

## WHEN YOUR SHIP COMES IN

The camel has been referred to as the "ship of the desert" in reference to the saying, "when my ship comes in." Good is coming your way! Isaiah the Prophet wrote, "Vast caravans of camels will converge on you, the camels of Midian and Ephah. The people of Sheba will bring gold and frankincense and will come worshiping the Lord" (Isaiah 60:6 NLT). This prophetic word was given in the Book of Isaiah to the people of God who were taken into captivity because of their rebellion. Their lives were devastated, but God gave them a promise. Large caravans of camels filled with wealth would converge on them.

God wants to speak promises into your heart and over your life. It doesn't matter about your past. God is the one who restores, and, through His forgiveness, you can walk in a life of blessings. You don't have to go out looking because the caravan of camels will overtake you. You don't need to search for blessings; instead, you need to seek the Lord. As you delight yourself in the Lord, He will give you the desires of your heart. (See Psalm 37:4.)

Your camels are coming! God's goodness and mercy will follow you all the days of your life. (See Psalm 23:6.) They will follow you through sickness, heartache, pain, and disappointment. You can turn around and see the goodness of God and His mercy as you look back at yesterday. Where can you go from the Spirit of God? No matter how high or low, still God is there. God is present with you, and His hand will continue to lead you, and His right hand will uphold you. (See Psalm 139:7-10.) Your ship is coming! Just keep your mind on Jesus and not the problems you are facing today.

## A GENTLE GUIDE

Gently He guides even in times when we ignore Him. Still he continues to gently pull us toward Him.

Patricia was having a very rough day. She called a friend complaining. *"I don't think anything is going to change for the better in my life."*

They had both attended the Bible study just a few days before where I had spoken about camels of blessings coming while meditating on Scripture. Her friend reminded her, *"Your camels are coming."*

Patricia felt the heavy weight of her problems. She thought, *"I need and deserve a pity party night."*

*"It doesn't seem like any camels loaded down with blessings are coming my way,"* she replied to her friend.

That night she lie in bed turning her problem over and over in her mind. Suddenly, she decided to take action. Purposefully, she turned her mind to the Scripture chosen for the Bible study group to meditate on for the week. *"For God is working in you, giving you the desire and the power to do what pleases him"* (Philippians 2:13 NLT).

She began to quote those powerful words over and over again in her mind. *"Yes,"* she began thinking, *"God is working in you, Patricia."*

As her mind began to calm, she began praying, *"God, I'm sorry for not trusting You. I'm sorry for having a pity party instead of meditating on Your Word."*

All of a sudden, she saw a picture in her mind. She saw herself, and she was holding her will and her way, but tied around her was a rope that represented God's Spirit. God was holding on to the other end of the rope.

He said, *"Don't worry, because I have you, and I am leading you. Even when you don't want to go with My will and My way – My Spirit draws you to follow me. When you feel tension in your life, it is you pulling against the rope wanting to go your own way, but know for a certainty that I have you. You are not going away or straying. The Holy Spirit is leading you. My Spirit will help you to come and follow My will."*

What a beautiful reassurance that God will gently guide us. Even when we make mistakes, His Spirit draws us to follow Him. When we insist on going our own way, we feel a tension. The Holy Spirit continues to gently lead us toward God's will for our lives. We can trust in Him.

# CHAPTER 7

## Scripture Meditation

**3 KEYS TO SUCCESS**

1. Speak it (Keep God's Word always on your lips.)
2. Think it (Meditate on God's Word day and night.)
3. Do it (Be careful to do everything in God's Word.)

*– Joshua 1:8*

### GOD SPEAKS THROUGH SCRIPTURE MEDITATION

Years ago, I was meditating on a phrase of Scripture from the Book of Matthew: *"...'You shall worship the LORD your God, and Him only you shall serve'"* (Matthew 4:10 NKJV). I heard God speak very clearly to my heart about an area in my life I didn't even realize was a problem.

I felt God saying, *"I am tired of you serving other people and looking to them for approval to see if they recognize that I have called you to ministry. Why don't you ask Me if I called you?"*

The Word of God became alive in me and pierced down to the deep insecure places in my life. As a music minister, I longed for approval from the pastors I worked alongside of. I wanted them to see that I was also called of God. It seemed the music ministry was placed on a lower level than the pastors' ministry. There was an invisible door that was closed when it came to being accepted as part of the pastoral team. There was a line drawn in the sand I could not cross. So I found myself trying to prove I was called of God. *Maybe if the worship was amazing, and if there was a powerful move of the Spirit of God, then they would finally realize my calling.*

God was speaking to me in the deepest part of my heart that was hurting by constant rejection. When I started meditating on the phrase, *"You shall worship the Lord your God, and Him only shall you serve,"* God's Word pinpointed an area in my life that needed to be healed. He spoke directly to me. It impacted the course of my entire life in just a moment.

Moses thought his brothers would understand God had called him, but it was a disappointment to realize they just couldn't see it. They even asked Moses who had made him the ruler and judge over them.

Joseph faced the same dilemma. His family thought his dreams were outrageous; they didn't realize they were from God. (See Genesis 37:18-20.)

David's father, brothers, and even the Prophet Samuel had a hard time comprehending God had actually called David to be the king. (See I Samuel 16:6-13.) So don't feel too bad if you are up against the same attitude by those around you. It is something many people face.

When God spoke to me, it was a defining moment in my life. I went to my knees and repented for my actions. I stood up knowing I was anointed and called by God whether anyone ever recognized it or not. Those few days of meditating on *"Worship God alone and serve only Him"* (Matthew 4:10), was revelation knowledge for my life. No longer did I need to battle with hopes that maybe the pastor would finally realize I was called of God. No more trying so hard. I could relax, because the opinion of others was no longer a driving force in my life. What a relief to get that burden off my back. God's Word came in a convicting but loving manner and opened my eyes to see where I was becoming a slave to men.

It was a personal word for my particular circumstance, but it also relates to everyone. Whenever we look to others for approval, we begin serving them, and it can become a trap. We are to serve God alone.

God wants to speak and tell you things you do not know. Scripture says God has placed something so great inside of you that you can't even imagine the great things God has planned. If it is beyond your imagination, then, of course, it is going to be beyond what other people can see. Even the ones who encourage you the most in your life cannot fully grasp what God has placed inside of you. It is too big for them to comprehend. You can't imagine it yourself. God's plan is wonderful! God wants to show you revelations, inspirations, patterns, and plans of how to accomplish the goals in your life. Look to God for approval. Serve only Him. Worship only Him!

## WE DON'T KNOW THE WAY

Jesus explained to His disciples that He was going to return to His Heavenly Father to prepare a place for them. "Thomas said to him, 'Lord, we don't know where you are going, so how can we know the way?' Jesus answered, 'I am the way and the truth and the life'..." (John 14:5-6 NIV). Sometimes I have felt like those disciples. I want to do what is right, but I just don't know which way to turn.

Turn your focus off your problems, because whatever you focus on will become magnified in your life. You don't have to worry and stress about trying to find the right direction. The answer is to simply look to Jesus and follow Him. He is the way, and as your attention and focus is on Him, then you will begin to walk in the right way, and everything else will line up.

I love the way the New Living Translation puts this question posed by Thomas, *"We have no idea where you are going, so how can we know the way?"* Often we feel like asking the same question, *"Where are you, God? We can't see, and we don't know where to go or what to do."* But listen to the confident voice of Jesus speaking into your heart today saying simply, *"I am the way!"* Follow Him, and you will get to where your life needs to go.

If you follow your dreams and plans, you may feel frustrated and disappointed, but, if you will follow Jesus, He can work it all out. He is the way! He is the way regardless of where you want to go. Stop your striving and sit to rest a while at the feet of Jesus. Listen to His words of wisdom. He is the way!

Turn your eyes on Jesus, and everything else will find its rightful place. When your eyes are on Jesus, it will change your whole outlook on life. It puts things in the right perspective so you can progress with confidence to make wise decisions. Don't focus on your problems; instead, focus on Jesus. Don't become preoccupied with your career; instead, keep your eyes on Jesus. Your world will be balanced as you lift Jesus up to His rightful place in your life.

## INVENTIONS

George Washington Carver was born into slavery around 1864. His exact birth date is unknown. He rose above racial barriers and became a scientist, educator, and inventor. His work at the laboratory in Alabama's Tuskegee Institute resulted in the creation of over 300 products from the peanut. His inventions include plastics, adhesives, shaving cream, and printer's ink to name just a few. He became one of the most distinguished inventors of his day. His secret of success was found in the Bible, "In all thy ways acknowledge him, and he shall direct thy paths" (Proverbs 3:6 KJV).

Carver said, *"All my life I have risen regularly at four o'clock and have gone into the woods and talked with God. There He gives me my orders for the day."* He held very few patents for his numerous inventions because he believed all of his ideas came from God, and he didn't feel at liberty to sell them. He said, *"I asked God why He made the peanut."* Then, with a handful of peanuts, he went into the laboratory with God and began to work. Carver believed he was a co-worker with God. The door to his lab was locked while he was creating because, when he was alone, he could draw close enough to God to discover His secrets.

Carver is an outstanding example of how to keep our focus on the great Creator. God is the source of all inspiration. He has the answer to all our problems. He alone can see the past and the future and how it all perfectly weaves together to form a beautiful design. Carver prayed and asked God to reveal to him secrets of nature, and we, too, can ask God to open up our minds with creative ideas. As Carver kept his thoughts on God's Word, he became smarter than those around him. He was given Divine insights others had missed.

God can show you things others overlook. God can open your eyes to see solutions for problems facing our world today. God is able to use you to invent and create products to help humanity. Turn your eyes on Jesus and let His thoughts fill your heart. Let His truth lead you and enlighten your path. The answer is looking to Jesus.

## CREATIVE POWER

God's Word has creative power. Positive thoughts are great and often line up with God's Word, but thinking on God's Word is so much more powerful. Positive thinking can enhance your life, but thinking on the Word of God can change your life forever. It is creative, life giving, destiny-changing with more power than you can even imagine. When you tap into the creative flow and power of God's Word, miracles can occur instantly. When God speaks, He can create something out of nothing. We read in the first two verses of the Bible, *"The earth was empty, without any shape and it was covered in darkness."*

Gen. 1:3 Then God said, and there was light.

Gen. 1:6 Then God said, and skies appear.

Gen. 1:9 Then God said, and dry land appeared.

Gen. 1:11 Then God said, and grass and fruit trees started producing.

Gen. 1:14 Then God said, and sun, moon, and stars began to shine.

Gen. 1:20 Then God said, and birds start flying.

Gen. 1:20 Then God said, and fish start swimming.

Gen. 1:24 Then God said, and cattle began to moo and dogs barked.

The first chapter of the Bible is often referred to as the story of Creation, but I think it could also be named "and then God said." God spoke, and the universe came into being. If God's Word created the universe, just imagine what God's Word can create inside of you. It can resurrect dreams, visions, and impart inspiration for creative ideas and inventions. God's Word can create something out of absolutely nothing. In the beginning God spoke! By His words the animals, fish, and birds came into being. God can create beautiful, restful, and peaceful places in your life with just a word.

Because God's Word is alive and creative, it can change your dark night into a sunny day. God can turn your situation around and produce good things out of bad things. (See Romans 8:28.) It's bigger than just thinking nice thoughts. It's more powerful than just thinking happy thoughts. When you meditate on the Word of God, it will change your life forever. The Word of God will set your life on a fast track course for the good life!

We read in the Book of Wisdom, "Listen to the words of the wise; apply your heart to my instruction. For it is good to keep these sayings in your heart and always ready on your lips" (Proverbs 22:17-18 NLT).

## GOD'S WORD LEADS TO INTERNATIONAL MINISTRY

Denise Glen and her husband, David, are the founders of Kardo International Ministries. I was privileged to meet Denise at a conference in Singapore where we were both ministering. She possessed a gentle spirit, and peace surrounded her. In Denise's book, Wisdom for Mothers, she shares how God led her in the expansion of her ministry. At the beginning, her vision was simply to teach the five women who attended her Bible study, but it grew to include women in neighboring towns. The vision continued to unfold as she asked God to let her ministry expand across the United States.

A prayer ministry was born, and all-day prayer meetings were scheduled once a month. As a result, her teaching ministry began to experience rapid growth. For five years, Denise prayed that her books would be translated into Spanish. She shared her desire with those gathered at one of the all-day prayer meetings. They fervently prayed for a door to open for a Spanish translation.

This was different than any of the previous prayer meetings. There was a divine urgency in the prayers, and it felt like Heaven was touching Earth. Within weeks, the necessary tools for a Spanish translation were provided, and the work began. Within another few weeks, she received an email from a church wanting to translate her materials into Russian for a missionary trip. She was awed by God's plans. Soon another email arrived from a pastor's wife in Korea who had come into contact with her ministry material. They had begun to translate Denise's Bible study for the women in Korea.

In the midst of this supernatural growth, Denise's husband was offered a job in Indonesia. She didn't want to leave her ministry headquarters in Texas. The ministry was soaring. They consulted with a wise pastor who advised them to investigate the possibilities of whether this was the leading of the Lord. They made a trip to Indonesia to help make a decision, but, when it came time to leave, they were still undecided. This was a critical decision that would affect both of their futures.

Together they sat down and began reading the Psalms. Her husband would read a Psalm out loud and then stop and ask if she had heard anything from God. Then she would read a chapter and wait to see if either of them had heard a direction from God. After going back and forth through several Psalms, Denise turned to Psalm 139. When she reached verse 9 through 10, she began to weep. She could not even finish reading the chapter. *"If I rise on the wings of the dawn, if I settle on the far side of the sea, even there your hand will guide me, your right hand will hold me fast"* (NIV). They both felt a peace and knew God was guiding them with His Word.

Before anyone knew of their decision to move, she received three emails asking for her teaching material to be translated into the Indonesian language. Their move to Indonesia was greeted with a wide open door of opportunity. Indonesian pastors invited her ministry into their churches. God led her and her husband through His Word. When they didn't know what to do, they turned to the Holy Scriptures, and it came alive to them and became a burning lamp to illuminate which path to take.

Her ministry has continued to grow, and now her books have been translated into 13 languages. God led her into a worldwide ministry. God's Word is filled with instructions for decisions we face. God's Word has the answers. His Word is filled with revelation and will guide us along the best path for our lives.

God's Word can give you direction for decisions you are making in your career choices. God's Word can lead you and show you which job opportunity to take. God has a great plan for your future, and, as you seek Him, you will find Him. Instead of stressing over which job to take, try just meditating and reading God's Word. As you focus on His words, peace will flood your spirit. God has promised to lead and guide us. He is interested in your decisions, and He wants to guide you in a beautiful path for your life.

## REST AND BE AT PEACE

God leads us beside peaceful streams and makes us to rest in green pastures. (See Psalm 23:2.) Take a deep breath and relax, because your God is leading you to a place of peace. I have found God keeps repeating His direction to me over and over. It almost seems like everywhere I turn I see what God is trying to communicate. When I open my Bible, Scriptures jump out at me with the same message I felt God tugging at my heart. The Psalmist wrote, "... *He guides me along right paths, bringing honor to His name* (Psalm 23:3 NLT).

I was asked to come to Singapore and Indonesia when they hosted their first Women Who Worship Conference. I had started Women Who Worship conferences six years prior in Canada. Two women on our prayer team in Canada were connected to this church overseas. I had already made one trip to Singapore and Jakarta, Indonesia, just six months before to minister in music at a World Prayer Conference.

I was excited to return and minister among the beautiful Christians I had met. However, my peace was somewhat shaken when I received an email informing me of our accommodations. They planned to billet us in one of the believer's home.

Let me explain why this would alarm me. I traveled extensively in my teens and through much of my adult life in different singing groups. I loved zigzagging across the country, but sometimes our accommodations left much to be desired. Many places we stayed in were beautiful and inviting, but some were scary and dirty. We rarely stayed at one church longer than a night, so it was easy to endure knowing we were packing our bags the next morning, but this trip to Asia was over a two-week period.

I usually stayed in hotels when I traveled to speak or sing. I was bringing my daughter, who was a young teenager, and my elderly mother. It was one thing for me to have to rough it for a couple of weeks, but I was concerned over the welfare of my mom and daughter. I knew Singapore was a very wealthy country, but Indonesia was not in the same category. When you travel to some countries, you have to be careful about the water, food, and security.

I was in a dilemma because I didn't want to offend the pastor, but neither did I want to stay at someone's house. I really began to worry about it. I prayed and asked God to work a miracle. *"God, please change their minds and let them email me back saying they decided to put us up in a hotel."*

I didn't know what to do. Should I email and politely say I preferred a hotel? I didn't want to hurt their feelings or appear ungrateful. I felt God was speaking to me saying, *"Relax, I will fight your battles."* (See I Samuel 17:47 & II Chronicles 20:15.)

God continued to speak to me throughout the weeks before I left. Everywhere I looked, it seemed I saw the word "relax." It happened so often it would make me laugh, because it became obvious God was trying to get my attention.

One day we were swimming and called to order a pizza. I opened the cover, and printed on the inside of the box in bold red letters was one word, "relax"!

I began to say, *"Okay, I will trust you, Lord, in this situation."*

The day finally came for us to leave, and, as we boarded the plane, I began to feel apprehension again. We had layovers in Japan and the Philippines. Such an amazing trip, but worry was clouding my joy.

I tried to speak words of faith, *"God, I know You are going to turn this situation around. I praise you, God, because, when we get there, they will have decided to put us into a hotel."* I kept claiming our accommodations would change before our feet landed on the ground.

We arrived exhausted after 20-plus hours of flying. People from the church picked us up at the airport and took us straight to the church where a prayer meeting was underway. Afterwards, they took us out to eat, and the entire time I am still saying positive words of faith. *"Praise God, You have turned it around, and now they will take us to a beautiful hotel."* I kept trying to claim it over and over silently in my thoughts.

Instead, they introduced us to the lady we would be staying with. We climbed into her car, and still I continued claiming something would change on the ride to her house. We pulled up to a high-rise building. It was the Four Seasons Condominiums across from the luxury Four Seasons Hotel. We stepped off the elevator onto the top floor. The doors opened, and we walked into the penthouse. The view from the living room was breathtaking. The ceiling to floor length windows held a panoramic view overlooking Singapore. In front of the windows sat a large black grand piano. As soon as we were settled, I sat at the piano and started writing this song:

*Rest and be at peace*
*For I'm the Lord your God,*
*And I am with you;*
*I'll never leave.*
*So rest and be at peace,*
*For I will fight your battles.*
*Trust me and believe.*

It was a beautiful home. We were happy to be there. I knew this would be a safe and comfortable place for my mom and daughter to stay. I was thrilled to discover we would be staying with the same family in Indonesia. The condo was their home away from home, but their main house was in Indonesia. My dread had turned into excitement. This was much better than a hotel.

Their home was like something you would see in a movie. A large, curving staircase wound down into the living area below. Maids delivered our clothes to our rooms freshly pressed along with fresh-squeezed fruit juice each morning. I felt like a princess in a palace. Security was not an issue, because they had personal security guards that protected the property. God taught me to trust His voice. I just needed to believe and trust Him when He spoke clearly to me that He had it all under control. I was worried about something that turned out to be a wonderful blessing.

God wants to guide your steps by His Word. He wants to speak words of comfort to your heart. He wants to communicate with you, and He often does that through the words found in the Holy Scriptures. Isaiah the Prophet wrote, *"Your own ears will hear Him. Right behind you a voice will say, 'This is the way you should go,' whether to the right or to the left"* (Isaiah 30:21 NLT).

God has a great plan for your future. He knows every intimate detail of your life. He knows the number of hairs on your head. The Bible reminds us God sees the sparrow that falls, and, if He cares for the birds, then He will surely take care of us. You can relax and know God can take care of every detail of your life. (See Matthew 10:29.)

# CHAPTER 8

## God's Word

**3 KEYS TO SUCCESS**

1. Speak it (Keep God's Word always on your lips.)
2. Think it (Meditate on God's Word day and night.)
3. Do it (Be careful to do everything in God's Word.)

*– Joshua 1:8*

**WISDOM IS AN ADVANTAGE**

God's Word gives you an advantage. You can have special insight into situations others do not have. It gives you wisdom on how to resolve conflicts and problems. It makes you look smart! The writer in Psalms declared, "Oh, how I love Your law! It is my meditation all the day. You, through Your commandments, make me wiser than my enemies, for [Your words] are ever before me" (Psalm 119:97-98 AMPC).

His Word is filled with revelation knowledge. The key is to meditate on His Word all day long, not just for a few moments randomly here and there. Deliberately turn your thoughts to Scripture.

## WISER THAN YOUR TEACHERS

God's Word is filled with knowledge and wisdom. As you meditate on it, you will gain valuable insight. There is a promise of deeper insight than our instructors because of meditating on God's Word. "Yes, I have more insight than my teachers, for I am always thinking of Your laws" (Psalm 119:99 NLT).

This is a road of wisdom that will set you higher than others, because you are thinking God's thoughts. His ways and His thoughts are so much higher. When you see things through God's eyes, everything becomes a lot clearer. As you meditate on God's Word, you see things from His point of view. It will make you wiser than people who depend on their own ability or knowledge.

## WISE BEYOND YOUR YEARS

When you exchange your thoughts to God's thoughts, you will begin to understand what people much older than you cannot understand. Once again in Psalms, we read about the benefits of meditation. "I understand more than the aged, because I keep Your precepts [hearing, receiving, loving, and obeying them]" (Psalm 119:100 AMPC).

God's Word will make you brighter than co-workers with more experience. It will open your mind to understand what others miss. God's Word gives you an advantage. It will set you apart. It will lift you higher and make you wiser. The wisdom of man does not measure up to the God of Wisdom. The Bible says, "The foolishness of God is wiser than human wisdom, and the weakness of God is stronger than human strength" (I Corinthians 1:25 NIV).

## UPDATED NEW EDITIONS

My daughter went to purchase her books for university. She tried to purchase used textbooks because they were considerably cheaper. One year, every course had an updated new edition. The updated versions, with all the latest research, often contradicted what was previously taught. My daughter is studying psychology, and when I mentioned something I had studied years before, she laughed. Only "quacks" thought like that anymore. Educators now laugh at the principles I was taught as fact. Many concepts taught as brilliant insights just years ago are now relegated to old wives tales. God's Word never changes. It has stayed the same through the ages, and it still is just as applicable today as it was centuries ago.

We find these words in Scripture, "The entirety of Your word is truth, And every one of Your righteous judgments endures forever" (Psalm 119:160 NKJV). God's Word is always true and always right. It never ends because it is eternal. Jesus said, *"Heaven and earth will pass away, but my words will never pass away"* (Mark 13:31 NIV). Great minds will come and go, but God's Word will endure. New theories will be taught and old theories discarded, and still God's Word stands unwavering and unchanging.

You can fill your mind with the powerful words of God. You can choose to think about the truths that will never change. God wants you to live an abundant life, and His words will guide you toward the best paths for your life. You are chosen of

God. As a child of the Most High God, you have access to His wisdom. You have the advantage.

## TAKE THOUGHTS CAPTIVE

As you meditate on God's Word, He will be magnified, and the problems in your life will diminish. It doesn't mean your problems will disappear, but they will not consume you. As you focus on the power of the Almighty God, then you acknowledge Him as the ruler of your situation. Your circumstances do not have control of your future.

If hurtful words have pierced your heart, then turn toward the Healer of broken hearts. Don't waste another minute allowing harsh words to control your emotions. The power of their words is limited to the access you give them to roam around in your heart. The more time you spend thinking on those hurtful words, the larger the wounds they can inflict.

The Apostle Paul wrote to the Christians in Corinth, "… and we take captive every thought to make it obedient to Christ" (II Corinthians 10:5 NIV). You are the only one who can control your thoughts. You have the responsibility to take action. There is a wise old saying, *"You cannot keep birds from flying over your head but you can keep them from building a nest in your hair."*

Thoughts can enter your mind, but you don't have to allow them to stay. You can think about something different. You can choose to think on the life-changing words of Jesus.

Don't let negative thoughts take up residence in your life. Evict them out of your heart and make a comfortable place to welcome the Holy Spirit to stay. The blessed person meditates on God's Word day and night, literally every chance you get.

Chew on it over and over again. Digest the living Word of God into your system. Think about how great your God is. Sing praises that tell of His marvelous deeds. Testify and speak about the miracles He has done in your life. "You will be like a tree planted by the rivers of water that brings forth fruit in its season. Your leaves will not wither and whatever you do will prosper." (See Psalm 1:3.)

## MARY VERSUS MARTHA

Mary sat at the feet of Jesus, but Martha was too busy. Jesus said, "... *Martha, Martha, you are worried and troubled about many things*" (Luke 10:41 NKJV). If you find yourself anxious and bothered about many things, then do an inventory to see if your focus is on the cares of this life. Come and sit at the feet of Jesus and listen to His words of life.

I know what Martha was busy with appeared to her really important and urgent. She had people coming for dinner, and an entire meal needed to be prepared, but, dear Martha, if you will listen, maybe you will hear about how 5,000 were fed with just a few loaves and fish. Martha is concerned about preparing a meal for the One who miraculously fed the multitudes.

Did she forget the stories of how God fed over a million people with supernatural nourishment with fresh manna from heaven? When they wanted meat, quail flew in, and they ate until they were sick. If you are living in the Martha syndrome, then you need to take some time to think about the miracles of Jesus and the mighty wonders of God.

Prayer and meditation can appear to be a waste of time to those who observe. Martha came to Jesus and said, "... *Lord, doesn't it seem unfair to You that my sister just sits here while I do all the work?...*" (Luke 10:40 NLT). If you make praying and meditating a priority in your life, there will be people who may accuse you of wasting your time. They may think you are just sitting around. I've heard it said, *"You can't just pray about it, you have to do something."* I know there is partial truth to that statement, but praying is doing something. Praying will accomplish feats you could never accomplish by your own strength. As you pray and God reveals what you should do, then you need to get up and do it.

If you will take the time to hear what Jesus has to say, then you will hear about the miracles, and the Martha focus will turn to awe at His power. It may not be necessary for you to be sweating, bothered and troubled about all the little things that need to be done in the kitchen, or even church work. You will stop being bothered by what others are doing or not doing around you. Take time to sit and listen to God's words, and you will see the stress of the day start to disappear. Make it a point to think on His words and see your whole situation in a different light.

The story ends with these words from Jesus, "... *Mary has chosen the good portion [that which is to her advantage], which shall not be taken away from her*" (Luke 10:42 AMPC). It is to your advantage to spend time in the presence of Jesus. It will benefit your future when you think on His words. There are multiple blessings associated with speaking the positive words from Scripture. God's words will give you a supernatural edge, because it can pierce right down to the heart of the matter and reveal hidden agendas. God's Word is filled with power.

## DAVID FACED GOLIATH

How can you face 'Goliath'? You can defeat the giants in your life by thinking about how big and mighty your God is. How did a little shepherd boy walk out and conquer Goliath? (See I Samuel 17.) His focus was on His God. Every giant will appear small when compared to the greatness of our God.

The others in the army were fearful and intimidated because they kept thinking about how big and powerful Goliath was, but David was thinking other thoughts. You can tell what they are thinking by what comes out of their mouth. They said, *"Have you seen this man?"* But David said, *"How dare this man speak against the armies of the living God."* (See I Samuel 17:25-26.) We can see two different focuses. One is focused on the enemy; the other is focused on God's ability and provision.

David's focus filled him with faith. While the rest of God's army shook with fear, David ran toward Goliath. While the others turned and hid, David is speaking words of victory before he even walks out to the battle line. (See I Samuel 17:11, 24.)

He was a man with supernatural faith. He had the kind of faith that grows by spending hours in the Word of God. David realized God was his source. The first sentence he speaks to the enemy is, *"You come to me with a sword, a spear, and a javelin, but I come to you in the name of the Lord of host, the God of the armies of Israel."* (See I Samuel 17:45.) He points out that the giant is using carnal weapons. Goliath is coming with natural things, but David is coming to fight in the supernatural power of the Name of the Lord of all Creation. He had the advantage, not because of his physical ability, but because of his source.

When your source is the power of God, then the battle is already won. As you place God's words continually before you, then you will see enemies fall to the ground as the banner of victory is raised in your life. Your thoughts and your words have tremendous power.

## ASK GOD TO HELP YOU LOVE HIS WORD

Some people find Bible reading boring, but my advice is to talk to God about it. He already knows how you feel, so there is no use trying to pretend. The benefits are so great. God can give you a love for His Word. Ask! God loves giving good things to His children.

As a teenager, I spent many hours in prayer. My pastor often started 24-hour prayer chains. They would usually fall apart after a few months, but I'm thankful he didn't get discouraged; instead, he would just start another one. We would take two-hour shifts in the prayer room at the church. There was a sign-up list with slots for each hour of the day. I signed up, but the people scheduled to come after me rarely showed up. As a young teenager, my time was usually flexible. As a result, I would spend three to four hours daily in prayer. It completely revolutionized my life. The more you pray, the more you are hungry to pray. I experienced this phenomenon and loved spending time in the prayer room.

One thing that troubled me was that I found the Bible quite boring. The main translation back then was the King James Version, and I found it hard to understand. I prayed and asked God to help me love His Word. It wasn't long before I started discovering patterns and key words or phrases in different books. It was almost like a puzzle, and I was discovering how wonderful it was. We read in the Psalms, "Open my eyes that I may see wonderful things in your law" (Psalm 119:18 NIV). Evidently it's a cry that has been prayed down through the ages of time. God can change your whole perspective and give you a deep-rooted love for His Word.

Another answer to my prayer came in an unexpected way. Our youth group started a Bible Quizzing team. We memorized entire books of the Bible, word for word. Our team traveled up and down the State of California to compete with other youth teams at local churches. The leaders organized tournaments, and memorizing God's Word became lots of fun. God began to open up my eyes as I read His Word, and it became so exciting for me that I could barely put it down.

## LOVE FOR THE BIBLE

I know many people struggle with interest in reading the Bible, but God is our source for everything! Just tell God about your struggle, and He can help you. Read the words of the prayer from the Psalmist who asked God for help. *"Turn my eyes from worthless things, and give me life through Your word"* (Psalm 119:37 NLT). God is able to turn your eyes toward the things that really matter. Ask God for help. True life is found in His Holy Word. God's words will not only change your life but will also lead you to everlasting life.

What a privilege to join in with the Psalmist and pray, "Make me walk along the path of Your commands, for that is where my happiness is found" (Psalm 119:35 NLT). Real joy is always found in God's presence. In His presence is complete fullness and overflowing joy. (See Psalm 16:11.) When His Word is continually in your thoughts, it will lift you out of the pit of despair. It's hard to have a pity party when you're in the middle of a praise party.

The benefits of meditating on God's Word are vast. The Psalmist wrote many prayers asking God to give him a deep love for His words. *"Give me an eagerness for Your laws rather than a love for money!"* (Psalm 119:36 NLT). He understood this was more precious than pure gold. (See Psalm 19:10 NIV.) In fact, nothing you can desire can even compare to it. God's Word is filled with divine wisdom and understanding.

What can compare to the wisdom found in God's Holy Word? We read in Proverbs that wisdom has more value than silver or gold. It is more valuable than beautiful expensive rubies. Wisdom offers long life in her right hand, and riches and honor in her left hand. (See Proverbs 3:14-16.) God's Word is wisdom. Treasure is found in the Word of God. As you meditate on His words, your spirit will unearth precious jewels waiting to be discovered. As you keep His words on your lips, you will speak with divine wisdom beyond your education or ability.

## GOD'S WORD IS FILLED WITH PEACE

Turn your thoughts on God's Word and let His Word flow throughout your conversation. Reject worry and doubt and run toward peace. It is found in Jesus. When you give more time to carnal and negative thoughts, they will have power to disrupt your life. A price tag will not be found on peace. It's outside the limits of what money can buy. Jesus is the Prince of Peace, and His peace is available for your life. You can't earn peace, but you can experience it. The less time you dwell on destructive thoughts, the less influence they will have on the decisions you make. God's Word can fill your life with peace.

## GOD'S WORD IS TRUTH

God's Word is Truth. We are instructed to bind truth around our necks. (See Proverbs 3:3 NASB.) Your neck controls the direction your head turns. To bind means to secure. When a person is bound, their movement is restricted. This is how our thoughts should be secured to God's truth. Our thought-life should be restricted from roaming freely to destructive thought patterns. Bind your mind to the mind of Christ. Let the truth of God's Word control your thoughts and direct your actions.

## GOD'S WORD BRINGS FAVOR

We are to write God's Word deep within our hearts. As a result, we will find favor with God and man, and find good understanding in the sight of God and man. It leads to a good name and reputation, and you can become a person of integrity who is highly esteemed. (See Proverbs 3:3, 4.) All of these are the benefits of filling your mind and your heart constantly with God's Word.

## BENEFITS OF WISDOM

The Word of God is Wisdom. It is the way of wisdom. This is the pathway to pleasure. This can revolutionize your future and transform your life starting today. It's available to anyone who grabs hold of it. There are no racial, gender, social, or economic barriers. This is for anyone who wants it. Here are some benefits for everyone who chooses to embrace wisdom. Happy, blessed, fortunate, enviable (Prov. 3:13 KJV, NLT, AMP)

4. Length of days, long life (Prov. 3:16 NKJV, NLT)

5. Riches (Prov. 3:16 NKJV)

6. Honor (Prov. 3:16 NKJV)

7. Highways of pleasantness, delightful path (Prov. 3:17 AMP, NLT)

8. Paths of peace, ways are satisfying (Prov. 3:17 NKJV, NLT)

9. Tree of Life (Prov. 3:18 NKJV)

10. Life to your soul, life to your inner-self (Prov. 3:22 KJV, AMP)

11. An ornament to grace your neck, reflects beauty (Prov. 3:22 NIV)

12. Walk in your way safely (Prov. 3:23 NKJV)

13. Your foot won't stumble (Prov. 3:23 NKJV)

14. Unafraid, go to bed without fear (Prov. 3:24 NKJV, NLT)

15. Your sleep will be sweet, sleep soundly (Prov. 3:24 NKJV, NLT)

16. Inherit honor, glory (Prov. 3:35 NIV, KJV)

As you turn your thoughts toward the wisdom contained in God's Word, you will reap the promises listed in the third chapter of Proverbs. Put His Word in your thoughts and in your speech through reading the Bible, meditation and prayer, singing spiritual songs, listening to sermons, and every way possible. This is one of the keys to living a successful life. Take control of your thoughts. Take control of your talk, and your actions will follow.

# CHAPTER 9

## *Truth Wins*

### 3 KEYS TO SUCCESS

1.  Speak it (Keep God's Word always on your lips.)
2.  Think it (Meditate on God's Word day and night.)
3.  Do it (Be careful to do everything in God's Word.)

*– Joshua 1:8*

### HEALING OF THE MIND

I met Sharon several years ago. We met for a coffee to talk about her new book. She was a beautiful woman, well dressed, and appeared to have her life totally together. I was surprised when she started sharing with me her story.

Sharon was admitted to the psychiatric unit of the hospital eighty times over a nine-year span. She was given almost 200 shock treatments and prescribed one medication after another. Nothing seemed to penetrate the deep depression she suffered. Her doctor diagnosed her with refractory depression, meaning she didn't respond to treatment. This only reaffirmed her feelings of failure. Now she felt she wasn't even a good patient.

Sharon had been a Christian her entire life, and, yet, she couldn't seem to overcome the darkness. Her pastor encouraged her to see a Christian counselor in a nearby city, and this was the beginning of a transformation in her life. After so many years of treatment, she went with only a glimmer of hope left.

Her new counselor led her through questions and then prayers to expose lies the enemy planted in her heart. Together they asked God to reveal the truth about the traumatic events that had happened throughout her life. Many lies Sharon believed about herself were replaced with the truth of God's Word. Sharon learned to listen and hear the voice of God.

Over the course of the next three months, she faithfully attended counseling, and her healing and recovery were remarkable. As she began to accept the truth that God had spoken over her life, she began to experience freedom from the depression that had ruled her for nine long years.

Sharon explained to me, the words God spoke were often similar to the same words many of her former counselors had spoken to her. They spoke of her worth as an individual, and the value she had to offer, but when she heard God speak, those same words brought healing. When you hear God speak, it makes a difference.

As she tuned her heart to hear the words of Almighty God, her soul was flooded with light, and the dark clouds of depression were replaced with the light of God's truth. God's words were like a balm to her spirit, and they healed her from the struggle of depression. Sharon L. Fawcett now travels and speaks about her freedom from depression, and has written an excellent book, Hope for Wholeness, the Spiritual Path to Freedom from Depression.

## THINK DIFFERENTLY

John the Baptist was preaching in the wilderness of Judea. He said, "... *Repent (think differently; change your mind, regretting your sins and changing your conduct), for the kingdom of heaven is at hand*" (Matthew 3:2 AMPC). The first words we read of John the Baptist are "repent"! Think differently!

It is still the same today. We need to change our thinking. If we want a different life, then it begins with a different thought pattern. We imitate what we think about. No one can see our thoughts, but we reveal some of them by our actions.

## GOD'S WORDS ARE FILLED WITH POWER

With all the benefits that come with God's Word, it's no wonder Scripture admonishes us to meditate on it. When we fill our minds with words of such great power, it can change us from the inside out. Meditate on God's Word and not on what someone else has said. There is nothing more life changing than filling your mind with the Word of God.

Reading Scripture is essential, memorizing Scripture is beneficial, but when you start to think on Scripture day and night, your life will be forever changed. If you change your thoughts, you will change the entire direction of your future. *"For the word of God is living and powerful,..."* (Hebrews 4:12 NKJV).

God's Word brings joy! (Jeremiah 15:16)

God's Word creates faith! (Romans 10:17)

God's Word lights your way! (Psalm 119:105)

God's Word brings healing! (Matthew 8:8)

God's Word will build you up! (Acts 20:32)

God's Word is a weapon! (Ephesians 6:17)

## GOD SPEAKS OVER HIS CHILDREN

We have all experienced painful events in our lives. Some face divorce, relationship issues, financial problems, abuse, or the loss of a loved one. During these dark times, we can choose to listen to the voice of God or the lies of the enemy.

Your Heavenly Father will speak words of comfort and reassurance to you. God will reaffirm His words: *"You are my beloved; I will never leave you or forsake you; do not fear for I AM with you."* If you let God speak into your situation, you will come out a stronger person.

The truth is, God loves you.

The truth is, God is your refuge and strength, a very present help in time of trouble.

The truth is, God walks with you through the valley.

The truth is, God is your defender.

God's voice will bring peace, joy, and love. He is close to the broken-hearted and rescues those crushed in spirit. God wants to speak into the hurt places in your life. God's words will encourage and strengthen. Let the glory of the Lord fill your thoughts and your heart. Take time to pray and listen to God speak over the hurtful periods of your life. As you are persistent in listening to His voice, you will have the fortitude to walk through the trauma as you hear His voice of comfort surround you.

## SPIRITUAL MOMENTS

A friend of mine told of a spiritual moment she experienced. She was attending a revival meeting. The power of God was so strong she couldn't stand and fell to the floor under the anointing. She felt God's power flowing over her. She could hear the minister speaking. Whenever he quoted Scripture, it felt like bursts of energy pulsating through her. She could clearly hear and understand the Scriptures being quoted, but as soon as he began to elaborate on the Scripture, the sound became garbled. Then he would read Scripture again, and once again she could understand what was said, and bursts of power would flow through her with the words. As he went back to expounding on the Scripture, it became garbled again to her.

Later, as she thought about this experience, she was awed by the power of God's Word. It became a reminder to her about how powerful God's Word truly is. It has the power to pierce through any situation, even holy moments.

## TEAR DOWN THE STRONGHOLDS

There are strongholds that need to come down. The Bible says, "For the weapons of our warfare are not carnal but mighty in God for pulling down strongholds, casting down arguments and every high thing that exalts itself against the knowledge of God, bringing every thought into captivity to the obedience of Christ," (II Corinthians 10:4-5 NKJV).

Whatever we give priority to in our thought-life is what we exalt. We lift up whatever thoughts we choose to meditate on. Guard against this trick of the enemy. Refuse to let his lies take precedent over God's truth. You are the only one who can control your thoughts. You own the real estate of your mind. Your thought factory is a secret place no other human has access to. You alone hold the key to your thoughts. Take care, because they are one of the most influential things that will influence your life, success, and future.

God's voice will guide you, correct you, and set you free from the lies of the enemy. The devil will lie to you about what happened and why it happened. God's voice will bring healing, but the enemy's voice brings condemnation. God's voice is filled with love and compassion, while the enemy's voice tortures you. Learn to turn your attention to the voice of God and keep your thoughts centered on what God is saying over you. If you are tormented by your thoughts, then it is probably not God speaking to you. God is love. God speaks peace. God's voice brings healing to the hurting, hope for the depressed, and strength for the weak.

## POWER OF LYRICS

It was March 1990 and another sunny morning in California. I pulled into the parking lot of the small Bible college where I taught music. I wondered where everyone was. The campus seemed deserted as I made my way to my office located at the back entrance of the church. The office I shared was isolated from the rest of the offices. There was a Christian radio station across the street where most of the offices were located. The Bible college shared the grounds and buildings with the local church. I began working totally unaware of the drama unfolding around me.

The youth had held an all-night prayer meeting. My office was located behind the platform of the sanctuary where they had met. A 16-year-old girl was visiting from Canada and had joined in the prayer meeting. Around 1:30 in the morning, she left the building to get something from her car. A few of the young people were standing in the glass-framed main lobby and watched as she made her way back to the church. There was a concrete courtyard in front of the main doors. They heard a muffled gunfire sound and saw her crumble to the ground just a few feet from the front doors. She had dreamed just days before that she was murdered by an executioner. She had shared the dream with a few of her friends, and now they watched in shock and horror as it happened in front of them.

It was a terrible tragedy. She had been shot in the head. It appeared the murderer was hiding in the bushes next to the front door of the church. The ambulance transported her to the hospital where she died a few hours later. There were no suspects and no apparent motive. No weapons were found. It appeared to be a random shooting.

I was alone in my office when someone stopped in and told me what had happened. All of a sudden, the beautiful day became frightening. I hadn't paid any attention to the unusual quiet atmosphere. The students and faculty were meeting together, and the police were still trying to locate the suspect. Fear filled my heart. I was terrified as I realized I had been working in my office totally unaware of the manhunt going on around me.

I felt a wave of panic wash over me. I don't know why the campus wasn't completely closed with yellow police tape around the crime scene. They were still searching for the gunmen, and no one knew if he was hiding in one of the rooms or offices in the buildings around the campus. I had just walked unknowingly into a crime scene.

Everyone was scared of what might happen next. People were crying and praying all over the campus. I gathered my belongings and ran out to my car. My heart was pounding. When I arrived home, I was so frightened all I could do was pace back and forth. The house was empty, and I was terrified.

I turned on one of my favorite worship albums. As the music filled the house, I began to breathe normally again. The artist was singing about magnifying the Lord and He will be magnified in your life. The words and music flooded my spirit, and peace filled the house. As I sang the song of praise and adoration to God, my mind was turned from fear and focused on the greatness of God. The change was tangible. Fear was replaced by faith.

It was one of the most dramatic changes in my feelings I had ever experience. To go from panic to peace was a beautiful transformation. The fear that had overwhelmed my thoughts was replaced by faith-filled words of truth.

I led the church choir the next Sunday morning. The place was packed, and I carried the peace I had experienced as I led the choir in singing peace over the congregation. Lyrics set to music have a way of communicating to the deep places in our hearts.

It was a revelation to me about the power of lyrics in music. The words we sing over ourselves can bring peace when they are filled with God's Word. Songs can become our prayers. Lyrics songwriters have written can express the deep longings of our heart. It's important what you are listening to. Words are powerful and even more powerful when they are combined with rhythm and rhymes. Melodies stick in our hearts, and we can find ourselves singing long after the radio is turned off.

## WHAT ARE YOU SINGING?

I held several Women Who Worship conferences through the years with amazing speakers. Many of them shared their testimonies. I remember one story vividly. Chrissy was raised in a Christian home. Her parents were pastors who loved and honored God. Their home was filled with worship and spiritual songs but she began listening to a different type of music. Her parents didn't realize how damaging and destructive it was, and the effect it was having on her attitude and decisions. The lyrics were toxic. She listened over and over and sang along day after day until the words became her reality. It wasn't long until she was acting out the words to the song.

She couldn't break the hold of the obsessive relationship with her boyfriend. Her life was on a downward spiral. She lost great job opportunities. She was broke and lonely. She became so miserable she considered ending her life.

Through the prayers of her parents and church family, she recommitted her life to the Lord. She is now a beautiful speaker and pastor's wife. I was amazed when she revealed the paramount influence music had had on her life's decisions. The lyrics set her on a destructive path. Listened to over and over, the song became prophetic in her life.

Fill your heart with songs that glorify God and teach His

Word. Watch out for songs contrary to the ways and commands of God. Music is a powerful way to meditate if the song is filled with the words of God. Have you ever listened to a song that filled you with faith? That is the kind of song you want going over and over in your mind.

What we listen to can get planted deep inside the fertile soil of our hearts. We know faith comes by hearing God's Word, so when we fill our ears with music based on God's Word and His principles, doubt and fear begin to disappear. When our thoughts are consumed with what God has to say, our feelings of insecurity begin to disappear. The opposite is also true. Whenever we fill our ears with the propaganda of this world's twisted culture, then destructive attitudes and practices can be the end result.

The Scripture says to put God's laws and words into your mouth. You will be doing yourself a favor when you sing songs based on Scripture. As you sing words that glorify God's ways, you declare blessings over your life and family. You will be putting God's Word into your mouth, and there are amazing promises associated with this action.

What kind of songs are you singing? Why sing destructive songs about how your wife left you for your best friend. Songs are so easy to pick up. Have you ever had a song stuck in your head for days? Songs are a form of meditation, and the lyrics get into our hearts. Sometimes you can even catch yourself singing or humming the tune at inappropriate times. It's difficult to control because the song is in you. Pay attention to the words of songs and what they are saying over your life and future.

## A DOUBLE BLESSING

You have the power to speak into the lives of people who surround you. Your words have the ability to lift up or tear down. The words you say can help someone who is struggling to get through the day. When we turn away from hurtful words and start using God's life-giving words, then we can be a voice to those in darkness. In Ephesians we read, "Don't use foul or abusive language. Let everything you say be good and helpful, so that your words will be an encouragement to those who hear them" (4:29 NLT).

We get a double portion when we speak uplifting words. Not only can we encourage others, but, also, our words wash over our own spirit. We encourage ourselves in the process. There is a biblical principle at work here. Give and it will be given back to you. As you give words of hope, you hear them at the same time. We take in the words we are releasing to others around us. It's like splashing water on someone. More than likely you will get wet.

The Bible teaches, "Let your conversation be gracious and attractive so that you will have the right response for everyone" (Colossians 4:6 NLT). Keep speaking kind and thoughtful words to others, and you will be blessed along with the ones you are trying to build up. As you give, you will receive. It's a biblical principle that works in every area of your life. If you want to receive more, than you need to give more. Make it a habit to bless everyone you meet with kind words. Speak words that build up, and refuse to say things that tear down another person. You have the ability to encourage or discourage. Every day life and death is set before you, and you can choose to speak words of life.

The way we say something will make a big difference in the

way it is received. Attitude comes across in the tone of voice that is used. The Bible tells us to speak the truth in love. (See Ephesians 4:15.) Truth sets people free. Fear is a constant companion to someone who is hiding something from the past or a wrong behavior done in secret. The devil is the one who brings torment, and he will jump on that fear and torment the person with the fear of being found out. Whatever is hidden or covered-up is an area that the enemy will torment the person with. Truth cancels the threat.

Sometimes people that have been exposed seem relieved. The lie was too heavy to carry. It seems they breathe a sigh of relief that it's finally out in the open. The consequences are often painful, but the weight of guilt can be debilitating. Walking in truth is the best option to live a successful life.

### Guard Your Heart

Words come at us from almost every angle. We hear words on the television and radio. Sitting in restaurants, you can hear conversations from surrounding tables. Walking down the sidewalk, words are being spoken around you. As you walk through the mall, words are coming at you through the PA system, people talking, and signs painted with messages. Words are everywhere, and they come at us layer after layer. Thousands of words every day pour into our subconscious. We can't control every word that comes into our ears, but we can control what words are planted into our hearts.

We have the power to uproot negative thoughts and words and not let them take root in our heart. The Bible says to keep your heart with all diligence, for out of it springs the issues of life. The New Living Translation writes, "Guard your heart above all else, for it determines the course of your life" (Proverbs 4:23). The words you allow to enter your heart can actually determine the course of your life. The direction your life will take is directly affected by the words rooted in your heart. Take inventory of all the negative news flashing across your brain and start deleting it.

The Bible has a lot of things to say about words. In the Book of Wisdom we read, "Avoid all perverse talk; stay away from corrupt speech" (Proverbs 4:24 NLT). Do this just like you would avoid catching the cold or flu. This is much more serious than a common cold. If you catch negativity, it can move your life down a road you don't want to get stuck on. Find people who are filled with faith and start listening to what they have to say. Fill your heart with God's words, and you will be filled with faith and hope.

If you are discouraged, check to see where it started. Did you allow yourself to listen to negative talk? Did you spend the evening watching negative news on the television? Did you allow your mind to wallow in self- pity? Guard your heart. Let there be some armored men on 24/7 rotating doing security checks. Don't leave yourself exposed to the tricks of the enemy who loves to come in and steal your joy and your peace of mind.

# CHAPTER 10

## Guard Your Heart

### ANCIENT SECRETS TO SUCCESS

1. Speak it (Keep God's Word always on your lips.)
2. Think it (Meditate on God's Word day and night.)
3. Do it (Be careful to do everything in God's Word.)

*– Joshua 1:8*

### THE BEAUTY OF THE LORD

I was talking with a friend recently, and the conversation turned to how young he and his wife looked. He remarked, *"Jesus is child-like, not childish."* They commented that people who grow in grace with God become more beautiful through the years. The beauty of God shines through them even when their body begins to fail. People who grow in the beauty of the Lord often appear younger because their spirit is young inside them. They have kept God at the center of their lives, and they are filled with positive wisdom that draws others around them.

This beauty that shines outward doesn't happen to everyone who calls themselves a Christian, but there are many who have filled their hearts with the love of Jesus, and it radiates on the outside. It is lovely to be around people who have guarded their heart. They have nurtured the good memories, and thankfulness is firmly planted in their heart's soil. Joy continues to grow from the thankfulness they sowed. People who have let bitterness grow in their thoughts and heart are not easy to be around. The bitterness always spills out, and it is not a pleasant experience.

My mother is one of those who guarded her heart. She suffered several small strokes a few years ago. Her mobility is limited. She can no longer drive, and she uses a walker to get around. Her days are often filled with doctor appointments, but there is a light inside of her that shines out. I have seen her take the hand of doctors and begin praying over them and their families. They tell her their family problems, and she prays for each family member individually. This is a beauty not diminished with sickness. This beauty is not skin-deep, but it is heart-deep, and it is an amazing thing to witness. My mother continues to grow in beauty and grace, and the pain in her body can't extinguish the flame of beauty that burns deep inside her heart. She is a joy and inspiration to be around.

Remember, it is what you think, how you talk, and what you do that will bring you onto the path of success in whatever you pursue. Fill your thoughts with wisdom and let your words be trained by wisdom, so your actions will result in wisdom. "Getting wisdom is the wisest thing you can do! ..." (Proverbs 4:7 NLT).

## FILLED WITH WISDOM

The Book of Proverbs encourages us to embrace wisdom. Listen to wisdom, pay attention and learn. God's Word is wisdom. His Light is like a floodlight that illuminates the right path to walk in. Fill your heart with His light and revelation. "Get wisdom; develop good judgment ..." (Proverbs 4:5 NLT). Search out wisdom.

Here are some of the benefits listed in Proverbs 4 for those who grab on to wisdom.

Wisdom will:

1. Protect you
2. Guard you
3. Promote you (make you great)
4. Honor you
5. Lead you in straight paths
6. Enable you to walk unhindered
7. Enable you to run and not stumble
8. Bring life
9. Crown your head with glory
10. Place beauty and grace upon you

"Jesus grew in wisdom and in stature and in favor with God and all the people" (Luke 2:52 NLT). We can grow in wisdom as we fill our thoughts with God's Word. As we grow in God's wisdom, our relationships with God and with other people will grow in favor.

## FEAR OF FAILURE TALK

Don't let fear talk you out of doing what God has called you to do. Fear has a voice, and it will tell you every reason why you shouldn't step out of the 'boat'. It's usually not logical. It doesn't talk to you from a realistic standpoint and makes mountains out of molehills. Sometimes it is so ridiculous that, if you stopped and really thought about it, it would make you laugh. Another thing you will notice about fear is it keeps exaggerating. If you listen to fear, it keeps growing and becoming more insistent. It doesn't just warn you and leave you alone. The more you listen to it, the louder and more insistent it becomes.

Perfect love casts out fear. Draw closer to the source of perfect love, and you will find the fear of failure vanish. Don't make decisions based on fear. Make decision when the peace of God has flooded your mind and heart. As you meditate more on the Word of God, you will be filled with wisdom. The Bible says, "From a wise mind comes wise speech;" (Proverbs 16:23 NLT). Wise decisions come from a mind filtered with God's Word.

Worry and fear will keep you tossing and turning all night long. Your mind will be hazy the next day from lack of sleep, but a mind stayed on Jesus if filled with peace. We find written, "You will keep him in perfect peace, Whose mind is stayed on You, Because he trusts in You" (Isaiah 26:3 NKJV). Keep your mind stayed on Jesus. He is the answer, He has always been the answer, and He will always be the answer.

When the fear of failure starts talking, drown out that voice with the voice of peace. God speaks peace to His children. He speaks peace over your life and family. He still speaks peace; be still in the middle of life's storms. He can still calm the winds and the waves. If your boat is tossing and turning in the storm of life, remember, Jesus is with you, and He has all power. We do not need to fear even if ten thousand fall on either side of us. (See Psalms 91.) In this day of rampant outbreaks of viruses, we can still our hearts knowing God is with us. We can walk in peace regardless of the state of the world.

The only fear you need is the fear of God. The fear of God is the beginning of wisdom. You can't even start down the path of wisdom until you have awe and reverence for Almighty God. We should be more concerned about what God thinks than what anyone else thinks. This is the way of peace, liberty, life, and happiness. No matter how hard the winds blow, and the storm beats against our home, it will stand because we are built on the Rock Christ Jesus.

## REJOICE ALWAYS

*"Rejoice always, pray without ceasing, in everything give thanks; for this is the will of God in Christ Jesus for you"* (I Thessalonians 5:16-18 NKJV). It is the will of God for you to have a grateful attitude. We should give thanks to God on a continual basis for what He has done for us. It is almost impossible to be grumpy and down in the dumps when we are thankful. A thankful spirit is directly opposite to a complaining spirit.

"Be anxious for nothing, but in everything by prayer and supplication, with thanksgiving, let your requests be made known to God;" (Philippians 4:6 NJKV). We don't have to stress out or let anxiety rule in our hearts. Our hope and trust is placed in our Heavenly Father. We can be thankful because we know God is on our side. What can man do to us when God is for us? Who can stand against us? It's God's favor following us every day of our lives with goodness and mercy.

## Health Benefits of Being Thankful

A friend shared an amazing story with me. Her mother was in severe depression. She was unable to eat and lost 100 pounds until she was literally skin and bones. She became so weak it was difficult for her to go from her bedroom to the couch in the living room. The family was desperately worried, but it seemed every treatment failed. Finally, they took her to a Christian psychologist who explained that their mother had lost the ability to be thankful. He suggested they take sticky notes and write down things she should be thankful for and paste them all over the house.

They posted small notes on her bathroom mirror, out in the hallway, on the fridge, and all over the house. She believed there was nothing to be thankful for in her life and quickly tore down all the notes. The family was devastated. They waited a few weeks and again posted the sticky notes of thankfulness all over her house. They were just little reminders like, *"I am thankful for my grandchildren,"* or *"I am thankful for food to eat."* This time her mother left the notes up. After a couple of weeks, the family saw improvements in her mental health. Within a few months, she was well enough to participate in family life. Her depression lifted, and she was able to function again.

Thankfulness is a powerful force that can propel us to a good place. It makes us realize what a blessed life we live.

## HEARTS OF PRAISE

We praise God, not only for all the material blessings that He has given, but for the spiritual ones as well. We are forgiven, set free, adopted into the Royal Family, heirs of the Heavenly Kingdom, and we have been given spiritual gifts and every spiritual blessing.

We are not victims, but we are victors through Christ who loved us and gave Himself for us (Galatians 2:20). We are winners, over-comers, and can do all things through Christ who strengthens us (Philippians 4:13). He has promised to be with us even when we walk through the valley of the shadow of death (Psalms 23). When the storms of life rain down on us, they will not move the foundation built on Christ the Solid Rock (Matthew 7:25).

We have peace like a river (Isaiah 48:18). We have an anchor in the storm. He is our Refuge and Strength, and a very present help in time of trouble (Psalms 46:1). When we remember what God has done for us in the past, it gives us courage to face today. Think about the wonders of God. Talk about the power of His name, and let your actions line up with the truth of God's Word.

## MAGNIFY THE LORD

The Psalmist wrote, "O magnify the LORD with me, and let us exalt his name together" (Psalms 34:3 KJV). When we magnify something, it doesn't make the object any bigger, it just makes it larger in our view. I need glasses to read small print, but when I wear my glasses, I know the size of the words doesn't actually change on the page. It's only my viewpoint that changes.

So it is with our thoughts. Whatever we think about and let our minds dwell upon always becomes bigger to us, because we magnify it by giving it our full attention. If we succumb to worry, our problems don't grow, but they appear bigger to us because we are magnifying them. It's just like putting a small molecule under a microscope. It doesn't grow, but it appears larger. Don't be fooled if a problem appears bigger because you keep thinking about it. Your view has made it bigger when, in reality, it's still the same size it was before you began thinking about it.

Magnify the Lord, and He will become bigger in your thoughts. It doesn't make God bigger. He already fills the universe, but when you meditate on Him, then He becomes bigger in your life. Your view enlarges so you can see more clearly. No matter how large your problems seem, they will never compare to His magnitude and greatness.

## OPPOSITION OR OPPORTUNITY

Joseph was sold into slavery, and the opposition he faced led to an opportunity of a lifetime. As he was led away in chains, every step he took was in the right direction for the fulfillment of the dreams God had given him. From Joseph's perspective, it would have looked like the wrong direction. He must have felt his dreams were annihilated with the betrayal of his brothers, but he realized in later years that, what they meant for evil, God meant for good. If someone has betrayed your trust, instead of thinking about what they have done, consider how God can turn your opposition into a great opportunity. Don't dwell on the hurt, instead, think about how God turned Joseph's situation around, and how He can do the same thing for you.

Joseph had the attitude of a winner. His thoughts were focused on thanksgiving and praise. We can get a glimpse of the way he thought through his actions. He named his first son Manasseh, which means to forget. God allowed him to forget all his troubles and hardships and the family who betrayed him. Joseph didn't live as a victim. He chose to leave the hurt and betrayal and not think about it. He was living in blessing and didn't want to be held back by the negative emotions that could destroy the joy in his present circumstances, and so, every time he called his first son's name, it reminded him that God had made him forget his past troubles.

His second son was named Ephraim, or double prosperity, because he said, *"God has prospered me in the land of my trouble."* (See Genesis 41.) His words point to a heart that was thankful.

Through faith, you can praise God in the middle of a trial knowing He has great plans for you. The Apostle Peter wrote to the church, "So be truly glad. There is wonderful joy ahead, even though you have to endure many trials for a little while. These trials will show that your faith is genuine. It is being tested as fire tests and purifies gold ..." (1 Peter 1:6-7 NLT). The fire of God will burn out the impurities in your life. So even in the midst of a trial, you can rejoice knowing you will come out stronger and purer as long as you keep your heart focused on God.

## BLESSINGS IN THE VALLEY

God's blessings overflow even when we walk through the valley. Whatever valley you walk through, God will provide everything you need. God leads us to a resting place and restores our soul. God prepares us a table, and we are invited to a feast spread out with the blessings of the Lord. While we partake of the table, all of our enemies can see how we are honored of the Lord. Our cup becomes so full it overflows. All of this happens through the darkest periods of our lives. It's a promise for the 'valley.' (See Psalms 23.)

The Good Shepherd will walk with you through the valley of death and make it a place of renewal and blessing. Here is another beautiful promise: "When they walk through the Valley of Weeping, it will become a place of refreshing springs. The autumn rains will clothe it with blessings" (Psalms 84:6 NLT). The Bible assures us God sees every tear we shed. "You keep track of all my sorrows. You have collected all my tears in Your bottle. You have recorded each one in Your book" (Psalms 56:8 NLT). God is with you. He walks with you. He speaks words of love to you. He cares about you and all that you are going through.

## TREASURE FOUND IN THE DARKNESS

Treasures of gold, silver, and precious stones are found hidden beneath the surface in the darkness; so is it with us in the spiritual. When we walk through times of grief and pain, there are hidden treasures we will find in the dark night. Don't fear the dark, because God is able to bless you right in the middle of the pain. Isaiah the Prophet wrote, "And I will give you treasures hidden in the darkness – secret riches ..." (Isaiah 45:3 NLT).

As a follower of Jesus, we can have peace beyond human understanding, joy unexplainable, and love that fulfills our every need. Everyone faces problems, hurt, grief, betrayal, and fears, but we can have joy right in the middle of our problems. "We can rejoice, too, when we run into problems and trials, for we know that they help us develop endurance. And endurance develops strength of character, and character strengthens our confident hope of salvation. And this hope will not lead to disappointment. For we know how dearly God loves us, because he has given us the Holy Spirit to fill our hearts with His love" (Romans 5:3-5 NLT).

One of the keys to success in our emotional health is to remember God's great love for us. The enemy will whisper all kinds of accusations that, if we are really loved by God, then this would never happen to us. We can rest on the truths that God is good and God is love, and He will never leave us or forsake us. You will never have to walk through trouble on your own. You have a source and a refuge. Remember to think about your Strong Rock, your Guiding Light, your Deliver, and your Provider.

Don't let fear crowd your mind. Let the peace of God flood your heart and mind. Let His love-filled words bring you the courage and faith you need to walk through the dark night. Has God ever let you down? Has God ever failed you? He is faithful and trustworthy. Fill your mind and your mouth with promises from His Word, and faith will arise in your heart. Hope will replace disappointment, and you will know God is going to bring you through for His glory.

## GREAT PLANS

God has a great plan for your life. "For I know the plans I have for you," declares the LORD, "plans to prosper you and not to harm you, plans to give you hope and a future" (Jeremiah 29:11 NIV). Your future is bright. You have a Heavenly Father with all the resources in the world at His fingertips. He owns the cattle on a thousand hills, and He is able to supply your every need and give you more than you can even ask or think.

Meditate on God's promises, and you will be filled with joy. "For the LORD your God is bringing you into a good land of flowing streams and pools of water, with fountains and springs that gush out in the valleys and hills. It is a land of wheat and barley; of grapevines, fig trees, and pomegranates; of olive oil and honey. It is a land where food is plentiful and nothing is lacking. It is a land where iron is as common as stone, and copper is abundant in the hills" (Deuteronomy 8:7-9 NLT). The Word of God is full of promises you can meditate on that will let your heart soar with faith. Our hope is built on Jesus Christ alone.

## MINDS STAYED ON JESUS

In the middle of the sinful and perverse activity around us, we can keep our mind stayed on our God, who is pure. He is totally pure. He is complete truth. He is always faithful. He is always just. He is a loving father. The nightly news is enough to bring fear to any heart. But we, as believers, are told not to fear but to lift our heads and focus on the truth that His coming is near. (See Luke 21:28.)

Lift up your head, because help is on the way. Lift up your head and let the King of Glory come in through the gates. (See Psalms 24:9.) He is the one who lifts up our heads. (See Psalm 3:3.) We don't have to walk around with our heads held low. He strengthens and lifts us up.

In the middle of wars and rumors of wars, we can have peace. We can remain calm knowing our hope is in Jesus Christ. "For God has not given us a spirit of fear, but of power and of love and of a sound mind" (2 Timothy 1:7 NKJV). We do not have to live in fear of the future.

When my daughter was in grade school, her teacher warned of grave devastation because of global warming. His version of global warming was illogical. One of her friends couldn't sleep at night. She thought the end of the world was imminent. I felt sorry for this poor young girl tormented because of a teacher who terrified his young students.

Our hope is in Jesus alone. Our hope is not in environmental cleanup but in the God who is the Great Creator. (See Genesis 1.) Our hope is not in the economy but in the God who owns the cattle on a thousand hills. (See Psalms 50:10). Our hope is not in the right elected official but in a God who can turn the heart of a king whatever way he chooses. (See Proverbs 21:1.) If you are stressed out, maybe your hope is misplaced.

I know my God is in control, and I don't need to fear any kind of disaster. I am determined to keep my eyes and my thoughts on how big my God really is. No evil in this world can stand up to the purity of God. No plan of the enemy can stop the plan of God in my life. No economy disaster can keep God from supplying all of my needs. No weapon formed against me will prosper. (See Isaiah 54:17.) No darkness can extinguish the Light. We are called to be the light of the world. Don't focus on the darkness, but focus on the Light!

# CHAPTER 11

## Healing Words

**ANCIENT SECRETS OF SUCCESS**

1. Speak it (Keep God's Word always on your lips.)
2. Think it (Meditate on God's Word day and night.)
3. Do it (Be careful to do everything in God's Word.)

*– Joshua 1:8*

**A DIFFERENT KIND OF PEACE**

Jesus said, *"Peace I leave with you, My peace I give to you; not as the world gives do I give to you. Let not your heart be troubled, neither let it be afraid"* (John 14:27 NKJV). This is a gift of peace of mind. It's a kind of peace the world cannot give us. It's different than any kind of peace that comes from talking with friends or counselors. This peace is beyond comprehension.

Jesus said, *"Do not let your hearts to be troubled ..."* (John 14:1

NIV). Don't let your heart become agitated and stressed. The peace that flows down from the Father will fill your heart and your mind. This is how we are successful with our emotional health. We look to Jesus who is the Prince of Peace. We think about His greatness, and we rest in the comfort of His arms.

In the Book of Philippians, we read that we are not to worry about anything. We are to pray about everything. We come to God and thank Him for all He has done as we tell Him what we need. Paul wrote to the church, "Then you will experience God's peace, which exceeds anything we can understand. His peace will guard your hearts and minds as you live in Christ Jesus. And now, dear brothers and sisters, one final thing. Fix your thoughts on what is true, and honorable, and right, and pure, and lovely, and admirable. Think about things that are excellent and worthy of praise" (Philippians 4:6-8 NLT).

## POWER OF WORDS

Paul and Silas were on their way to a prayer meeting when the enemy sent a diversion to obstruct their path. A young slave girl with the fortune telling spirit started following them. Day after day she trudged behind them yelling out, *"...These men are servants of the Most High God, and they have come to tell you how to be saved"* (Acts 16:17 NLT).

This young girl was using her words to interrupt what the apostles were trying to do. What she was saying was true, but she was causing a scene and diverting attention from what they were trying to accomplish. I find it interesting the enemy sent someone using words to try and trap them. Many times we can be distracted by words. We can be on our way to do what God has called us to do, but something someone says can cause us to become sidetracked.

Paul was getting exasperated until, finally, he turned to her and said, *"In the Name of Jesus, I command you to come out of this girl."* (See Acts 16.) Immediately, the fortune-telling spirit left her body. The enemy attack came through words, but we have the Sword of the Spirit, which is the Word of God. So with words, the enemy attacked Paul and Silas, and with the words of Jesus on their lips, they defeated the enemy.

Of course the enemy sent another attack. Her owners were furious and dragged Paul and Silas to the city center accusing them of disturbing their city. They were beaten and thrown in prison without a trial. It seemed like the enemy had, indeed, won this time. Their feet were bound, their backs were bleeding from a beating, and they were in high security in the inner-most-part of the prison. It seemed like the whole city was against them.

Once more their words defeated the enemy's plans. Around midnight, they began praying and singing hymns. As the words of praise left their lips, the enemy's plans were defeated.

All the other prisoners could hear them singing. I imagine they were quite boisterous. They weren't intimidated. They didn't seem concerned with the late hour of night or worried about waking up any of their neighboring prison mates. As this loud worship was resounding through the prison, it was also resounding around the Throne Room of Heaven. God sent an earthquake, and the chains fell off their hands and feet, and the prison doors burst open.

The exciting part was, it wasn't just for their deliverance, but the prison doors fell open for everyone around them. Your words will influence your circumstance, but a side benefit is for everyone around you. Your words of praise can help your family, friends, and even people you don't know who just happens to be in close proximity to where you are. This is what happened in this story. The other prisoners' lives are being changed, because they are around two men who are using their words to bring the power of God down into the prison dungeon. (See Acts 16.)

The power of words formed into praise can tear down the walls holding you back. We are instructed in Scripture to be thankful for everything and to pray continually. (See 1 Thessalonians 5:16-18.) As we open up our mouths filled with praise, chains that have us bound will break. As we turn our thoughts to being thankful, our outlook in life will be different. As we concentrate on the good things in our lives, then the things irritating us will be reduced to an insignificant role.

Thanksgiving can still destroy the chains of defeat in your life. Turning your heart and mind to praise can still open doors so you can walk through to victory over depression. Turning your thoughts and words to praise can change your circumstances, and everyone else who is around you will be blessed just by being near you.

You have a great opportunity to not only change your future but to bring a blessing to your friends and family. God has enough blessing for you and the person next to you. In the middle of the dark night, Paul and Silas began to sing, and their dark night was interrupted with the miraculous. They turned their face away from their problems and turned their focus onto Almighty God. They began praising Him knowing He works all things together for our good.

## WORDS INSPIRE

"A word fitly spoken is like apples of gold in settings of silver" (Proverbs 25:11 NKJV). God wants to fill your mouth with encouraging words for those around you. The words of the godly are of great value, and the writer of Proverbs compares the words of the godly to pure silver. (See Proverbs 10:20.) You have been given the gift of choice. You can use your words to inspire others. You can use your tongue to uplift those around you.

It's wonderful to give good advice, and it's a great feeling to say the right thing at just the right moment. (See Proverbs 15:23.)

## WORDS HEAL

Many of the things we spend hours worrying about either never happen or turn out to be so insignificant we can't even recall the details. Sometimes, though, a problem or heartache comes that is so massive it can knock us off balance. It is usually in those moments that all of life's priorities come into sharp focus. In a matter of seconds, every dream and ambition can change because of the sorrow we are experiencing.

If you are going through something traumatic, you will need to give yourself time to mourn. But, even in the midst of agonizing grief, joy breaks through in unexpected moments. Once again joy starts to fill our lives. You can smile again. You can feel joy once again. There is always the rising of the sun. No matter how dark your night may be, remember the sun will shine again. The Bible tells us God is the God of all comfort. Turn your heart and thoughts to the promises of God because in them is life, and in them you will find comfort, joy, and peace.

People sometimes advise us to not quote Scriptures to people who are hurting, but, I ask, *"Where can you find more comfort than the words of God?"* When you don't know what to say, God's Word can give you the wisdom you need in that moment. The problem arises when we use God's Word to condemn someone who is mourning. Then we become like Job's comforters who bring accusations and blame the person for the problem.

The Prophet Isaiah wrote these words, "The Sovereign LORD has given me His words of wisdom, so that I know how to comfort the weary …" (Isaiah 50:4 NLT). When you feel lost for words, just listen closely believing God will give you His words to comfort those who mourn. Let God direct you during times of great sorrow. God's Word is filled with comfort and strength for the brokenhearted. We read in the Book of Wisdom, "The words of the godly encourage many …" (Proverbs 10:21 NLT). God has placed inside of you the ability to speak wise words to lift the spirits of those in grief. Again we read, "… the words of the wise soothe and heal" (Proverbs 12:18 TPT). You can be filled with the wisdom of God's Holy Word.

God can give you the words to say. God can bring a Scripture to your mind that will flood hearts with hope. Don't be afraid to use Scripture. It is powerful and has power to heal. God sends forth His Word and heals. (See Psalms 107:20.) It is important to use verses that encourage and not use verses as weapons that will injure those already in pain. You are equipped to be wise. Who has more wisdom than those who are led by the Spirit of God? Don't say, *"I don't know what to say."* God has promised to give you the right words, and you can open your mouth and bring encouragement and comfort to those around you. God can use you to help heal the brokenhearted.

## REAL ESTATE OF YOUR MIND

Negative thoughts destroy self-confidence. Reserve the prime real estate of your mind for God's Holy Word. Let His Word build a large dwelling place in your thought-life. Bright ideas and inspired plans will grow, as you allow God to have preeminence in your thought-life. The negative things will be resigned to a place of insignificance.

## IMPORTANCE OF YOUR THOUGHTS

Your thoughts will rule your heart, and your heart will rule your actions. If you are thinking the right thoughts, then you will make the right choices. It starts with what you think. We make choices based on our thought processes. What we think is right or what we think is wrong affects all of our decision-making.

Every great invention starts with an idea or thought. Just like the enemy plants in our minds negative thoughts, so the Creator of the Universe gives us good thoughts. Where do brilliant ideas come from? Where do ideas come from for books that change the world for the better? The thought comes from our Great Creator. He is the giver of wisdom. Great ideas can be downloaded into our hearts. He gives us the desire to reach out and to make a positive impact in the lives of those around us.

Don't worry about the negative thoughts of the enemy; instead, focus on the good thoughts God is speaking to your heart. Look for the Divine thoughts and treasure the inspirational moments. Pay attention to the quiet whispers from the Lord. Who knows what God will drop into your heart to develop? God could give you an ingenious invention to help people around the world. God wants to use you and bless you.

Allow the Holy Spirit to work through you. Let Jesus rule over your heart and mind, and, in so doing, you will reap wonderful benefits. The writer in Psalms reminds us not to forget the benefits of the Lord. (See Psalms 103:2.) His plans are to prosper and not harm you. His thoughts are to give you hope and a future. The life God has designed for you is full of the blessings of the Lord; so pay attention to what God is saying.

What He speaks will bring life to every situation you experience. When God speaks, it will illuminate every dark place you walk. Seek after God's thoughts. Look for God-inspired ideas. Listen closely with your heart and treasure what He speaks to you.

## FILL YOUR THOUGHTS WITH GOD'S WORD

Here are God's guidelines on what to fill our minds with. He is our Creator and knows the best way for us to function. "Fill your thoughts with my words until they penetrate deep into your spirit. Then, as you unwrap my words, they will impart true life and radiant health into the very core of your being" (Proverbs 4:21 TPT).

Then again we read, "Let the word [spoken by] Christ (the Messiah) have its home [in your hearts and minds] and dwell in you in [all its] richness ..." (Colossians 3:16 AMP). The path to success in every area of your life is to fill your mind with heavenly thoughts. When you keep your thoughts centered on God's greatness, it will encourage your soul. When you remember what God has done for you in the past, it will give you the courage to face your future. Fill your thoughts with God's Word.

King David wrote in the Psalms, "Let the words of my mouth and the meditation of my heart be acceptable in Your sight, O

LORD, my rock and my Redeemer" (Psalms 19:14 NAS). This beautiful prayer of David's is a cry to please God in the way he spoke and in the thoughts that filled his mind. We, too, can pray that God would help us to fill our mouths and our minds with the things that are pleasing to Him.

## HANNAH'S DESIRE

The Bible tells us God will give us the desires of our heart. God will actually place good desires within our heart. In the Bible, we read of a woman named Hannah. She was desperate to have a baby. She cried out to the Lord to open her womb. Even her husband couldn't understand her deepest longing, but she refused to be deterred. She had a desire burning on the inside of her that could not be quenched.

Hannah entered the temple of the Lord and began crying out to God in prayer. Her distress is so deep it's beyond words. She finds peace through prayer, and prophetic words fill her heart with hope.

Her prayers are answered when she gives birth to a son named Samuel. He became one of the greatest prophets and judges that ever ruled in Israel. He anointed Saul and David to be kings over Israel. What others thought was a selfish ambition on Hannah's part was actually a desire placed there by God. Israel was in dire need of a righteous leader to arise. The spiritual leaders were wicked and taking advantage of God's people. Samuel brought change to the priesthood and banished the corrupt practices. Samuel was trained to listen to God's voice.

The desire of Hannah's heart was much bigger than she could imagine. There may have been times Hannah felt selfish for her persistent cry for a baby. She didn't realize God was birthing an incredible work through her. The child she prayed so diligently for would become a holy leader in Israel. Her many prayers for this yet unborn baby would result in a baby surrounded by the prayers of his mother. Samuel would enter into ministry at an early age. He became a spokesman for Jehovah God.

## GODLY DESIRES

There may be something that stirs a fire inside you. Maybe you are passionate about helping people. You may feel deeply the hurts and wounds of others. God is working in you and through you. Not only is God transforming your life, but, also, He will touch many lives around you even though you can't see the whole picture. Your God-given passion in life is much bigger than what you can think or even imagine. Your deepest desires may be something to further the Kingdom of God. Don't be surprised if others don't understand why you have a driving passion. You probably can't explain it yourself, so don't expect others to see what God is doing in your life.

Great things are hidden in the darkness, and, usually, they don't come to light until they mature. The seeds planted are beneath the surface where others cannot see the growth. It is only when they begin to mature and grow that others around you will be able to see what God has called you to do. I believe God has called you to do great things. God has called His church to greater things. God has called you to do greater things!

### Looking Down in Love

There is a song we used to sing in Sunday school when I was a little girl. It was an action song, but it was filled with ancient truths. One of the verses began with, *"O, be careful little mouth what you say!"* We would point to our mouths as we sang those words. Another verse said, *"O, be careful little ears what you hear."* Each verse ended with the phrase *"There's a Father up above looking down with tender love."*[1.] What a beautiful reminder; God looks upon us with love. He hears every word and He knows every thought. The Bible tells us He knows what we are going to say before we even say it. (See Psalms 139.) He knows everything about you. God is involved in the minutes and seconds of your life.

## THE GREATEST SUCCESS

The greatest success we will ever experience is when we stand before the Throne and hear the words, *"Well done, good and faithful servant."* Our highest goal should be to live in a way that brings honor to the name of Jesus. To leave a legacy of a person who followed God's voice will be an ultimate achievement.

Jesus has a great plan for your life. Every command found in His Holy Word is for your benefit. His way is the road of wisdom. Jesus is the one true living God. He is the Way, the Truth, and the Life. Everything we need to live life to the full is found in Him. In His presence is where we experience complete and total joy.

I challenge you to fill your thoughts with God's Word, and to allow your mouth to speak His words. As you begin to meditate day and night on God's Word, you will experience abundant life. What you think about will come out in what you are talking about. What you think and talk about will affect every decision and action you take. You will be headed on the path to success. These are the Ancient Secrets of Success.

1. Oh, Be Careful Little Eyes – Public Domain, Author Unknown

www.ingramcontent.com/pod-product-compliance
Lightning Source LLC
Chambersburg PA
CBHW070244190526
45169CB00001B/302